ACKNOWLEDGEMENTS

Thank you Holy Spirit for incredible adventures! What an absolute privilege to partner with You in these amazing days!

Thank you Colin for believing in me and releasing me to work the long hours required to finish this project. You are an amazing husband, best friend and father of our two beautiful children.

I would also like to thank my remarkable team of Light and Life volunteers. You inspire me so much, and I love partnering with you for the Kingdom! Special thanks go to Ruth for your help with editing, and to Michael for creating some fantastic graphics.

I owe so much to Brian and Iris Gooding, Alan McWilliam, Steven and Helen Anderson and Jean Black. Your on-going support, encouragement and spiritual oversight are invaluable.

'The army's rising, the Kingdom's advancing, and history's being made.'

His forever,

Barbara

ENDORSEMENTS

Barbara, this is a phenomenal book! I really do believe that it is a clarion call to the Saints to rise up and step into everything that The Lord has for us to do. Thank you!

There is a new missionary movement arising within the church in these days. As with all movements there is a need for champions who encourage everyone else to press forward - Barbara Jenkinson is one such champion!

In *'Reaching Spiritually Hungry People'* Barbara has produced a roadmap to connecting with the 'white harvest' that Jesus promises. It will be hugely challenging for some who will have to throw off their church based paradigm to be able to first understand then embrace this missionary based paradigm. For those who have taken even the first few steps on this journey this book will make sense of their experiences and validate their 'hunches'.

I strongly and warmly commend this book as a key text for those who are thinking, praying and working to see the great white harvest brought in.

Alan McWilliam
Primary Leader, Whiteinch Church of Scotland
Chairman, CLAN Gathering

A while ago I was involved in an outreach where I talked with a lady who was on a spiritual search. She told me that she used to go to church, but now she was looking for something spiritual so she had left the church and was attending new age or psychic fairs.

Now many churches do of course offer something spiritual, but a growing number of people – young and old, male and female - don't recognise this. Despite being on a quest for spiritual answers and experiences, the last place many of these people consider looking to is to the church. This is the situation and opportunity that Barbara addresses in this book.

Out of her own experiences where she has seen much fruit, Barbara highlights the opportunities (as well as the dangers) of the rise of interest in other spiritualties. There is a harvest field that is waiting on Jesus' disciples to be thrust out and introduce searching people to Him. Barbara brings clarity, challenge and easy-to-follow practical guidance to help her readers reach out lovingly and powerfully to those who are on spiritual journeys that have so far missed the true source of life, Jesus Christ.

Some Christians get panicky when we start talking with language that enables meaningful engagement with those who are open to all sorts of spirituality, but we must do this if we are to connect to and help people find the truth in Jesus.

Barbara's ministry has always been Christ-focussed and centred, bathed in prayer and worship of the Lord, and led by the Holy Spirit. The on-going fruit of her ministry, and of this book, will be increasing numbers of people coming to a true encounter with Jesus Christ as Lord and Saviour.

In summary, I found this book to be inspiring, challenging and really good!

Steven Anderson
National Director, Healing Rooms Scotland
Senior Leader, Church Alive (Glasgow)

I have had the privilege of being envisioned, built up and released by Barbara Jenkinson. I have never encountered such a unique blend of humility, Godly character, purity of heart and Holy boldness. Where God moves she follows, her heart's cry burns with a passion for the Kingdom of God to be advanced on this earth. Barbara is a visionary and a strategic leader in our nation. Her heart is simply to see God's Kingdom and presence released wherever He leads her.

Barbara thrives in finding the gold in people, calling it out and bringing people into a place where they know who they are in Christ and can walk into all that God has made them to be. She works with a diverse group of people in Light & Life, encouraging and developing unity, building a community that loves and supports one another, centred at the core, regardless of background.

She has a passion and love for the Father, His Word and Holy Spirit working in unison that gives a balance and grounding to all that she does. She is totally committed to following the Jesus model of life, and spends hours saturating in the Word of God, soaking in His Spirit to gain fresh strategies, revelation and direction.

Her heart for the lost children of God is infectious. This book demonstrates her love and passion for 'those who are searching' and also of her unwavering commitment to walking with them to see the fruit God has destined for their lives come to fruition. As you read it, you will experience a fresh fiery passion for reaching the lost. You will also find yourself better equipped to use biblical tools to demonstrate God's abundant love to them in ways that are relevant, and that bring life changing encounters.

'*Reaching Spiritually Hungry People*' is an awesome read. Every Christian and church who wants to reach out effectively to today's society needs to get a copy!

Ruth Hart
Office Manager, Light & Life International
Administrator, CLAN (New Wine Scotland)
Office Manager, More Than Gold 2014

One of the many things I love about Barbara is her beautiful quirky sense of humour. She is an absolute joy to be around. Over the last few years Barbara has become a very dear friend to me, as well as someone I look up to. She's a constant inspiration, and oozes the presence and the love of Jesus in an almost tangible way. Barbara is one of my modern day hero's, a passionate, sold out, devoted woman of God who dares to go where others wouldn't.

'*Reaching Spiritually Hungry People*' is an amazing book. I know it will equip many people to be able to share God's love with others much more effectively.

Lennie Holt
Director, Ark Theatre, and Fusion Theatre Arts.

CONTENTS

INTRODUCTION

*R*eaching spiritually hungry people is an invitation to help usher in one of the largest moves of God this world has ever seen! The scene has been set, and the spiritual atmosphere lies pregnant with incredible possibilities.

On one hand society appears to be moving at warp speed towards secularisation, as church attendance plummets, and fewer and fewer people identify themselves with institutionalised religion. Yet in the midst of that, 'life has found a way' and a phenomenal revolution is taking place causing the spiritual landscape to be utterly transformed.

Ordinary men, women and children are experiencing an 'awakening' and becoming aware of the spiritual dimension surrounding them. In response, many are looking in all sorts of places for solutions to the hunger they feel inside.

Yet everything they need can be found through a saving relationship with Jesus Christ.

The opportunities that exist within this spiritually-charged climate are phenomenal, and Heaven has released a clarion call to the Church to arise and demonstrate the Kingdom of God to a spiritually awakened society through love, power, signs, wonders and miracles.

The days we live in are similar to those of Elijah, where it is the 'god' who answers by fire who will be declared 'God'. Today's seekers are not interested in words, arguments and intellectual debates, but in 'authentic' spiritual encounters.

As many have encountered the raw, undiluted Power and Presence of the Living God, they have gladly forsaken alternative spiritual paths and joined the growing throngs of those keen to explore what it means to be a follower of Jesus.

Our challenge, is to bring seekers into such encounters through the Holy Spirit. However, the prospect of ministering to people, with alternative spiritual backgrounds[1], can be daunting.

In this book I provide keys that will help you:

- recognise the spiritual revolution that is taking place, and the Kingdom opportunities generated;
- understand the language spiritual seekers use, and gain a greater understanding of the things they are looking for;
- learn to build bridges with seekers and bring them into encounters with Jesus; and
- discover ways to help them transition into Kingdom disciples.

As I have researched and written this book, I have become more convinced than ever that the Church (as described in the Book of Acts) holds the solutions needed to address the issues

---

[1] Which are most people in society!

that grip our communities and nations. However, for us to be recognised as a vibrant, dynamic, powerful force, we must first learn to communicate with the world around us and the people in it. I hope this book will help us do that.

I have written it as a resource for personal instruction, and also as a tool that can be used by groups and churches. Packed with true and inspiring stories, each chapter contains review questions and activation exercises.

But before you turn the pages, let me pray for you…

> *"Father , I thank You that the person reading this book is someone You have hand-picked to be an influencer for Your Kingdom. As they read through each chapter, let a fresh fiery passion for You and Your Kingdom arise in their hearts.*
>
> *Root them, ground them, and establish them in Your love. Let them see through Heaven's eyes, and teach them to operate from a place of love and intimacy. Baptise them afresh in Your Spirit and let them arise drenched in Your incredible love and power.*
>
> *Thank You that You have called them for such a time as this, to join the swelling ranks of revivalists that will see Your Kingdom released across every sphere of society. Thank You that they are called to help write our future's history."*

Chapter One

GET READY FOR A
REVOLUTION!

'They're queued all the way to the stairs and beyond!'

This was a comment, made by one of our astounded
Light & Life[2] volunteers as we prepared to hold an
outreach event at a city-centre hotel in Glasgow. They
were stunned by the sheer volume of ordinary people who had
come along, and as the doors opened, over 200 folk poured
into the room.

These were not church goers, but ordinary men, women and
children who had become desperate for a spiritual encounter
which would bring meaning and direction to their lives. For
many, it was their first encounter with Jesus, they'd simply
seen our advertisements in the press and come along, hoping

---

[2] Light & Life is an evangelistic ministry that combines creative gifts with
prophecy and healing to bring people into encounters with the Holy Spirit.

that something they would experience would meet the empty ache they felt inside.

As our volunteers ministered to them, tears flowed, and an infectious epidemic of smiles was released in the room. Eight of these precious people went on to ask Jesus into their lives, and many others were so impacted they left keen to find out more about the God who had just broken into the reality of their 'world'.

Many of the volunteers on team that night were ministering with us for the first time. It was an evening they are unlikely to forget. A young man on the healing team testified:

> *"We had so many healings I can't remember them all…! A lady came with sciatica and severe pain in her knee and back. We noticed one of her legs was shorter than the other, so we prayed for it. It grew so much we had to pray for the second leg to catch up! Her back and knee pain totally disappeared!"*

An excited woman from the massage team shared:

> *"We had a salvation in the massage team! As I was ministering to this young girl, I kept getting the word 'torment', and eventually asked her 'do you feel tormented?', 'Absolutely!', came the reply.' After praying God's peace into her, the feelings of torment left. Within a few moments, she had asked Jesus into her life!"*

These are just two short stories from a night packed with signs, wonders and miracles. This was just one of many such outreaches where we have found ourselves inundated by hoards of spiritually starving people, desperate to find hope and direction.

PROPHETS OF DOOM

For decades, academics have predicted the demise, and eventual extinction of 'belief in God' and 'spirituality'. For a while, it looked as though their 'prophesies of doom' were being fulfilled. Society became more and more secularised, and church attendance continued its downward spiral.

Yet, in the midst of this dark cloud, something incredible has been happening.

People are starting to realise the pursuit of happiness through material security, education, family, sexual fulfilment and escapism is failing to satisfy the deep inner cries of their hungry hearts and are looking for ways to fill the spiritual void they feel inside. This 'spiritual awakening' is impacting people from all different backgrounds and ages, and spanning every sphere of society.

THE FLOOD WATERS ARE RISING

In recent years, there have been so many reported incidents of people having spiritual encounters, that some of the same academics who predicted the death of 'religion and spirituality' have established university departments to monitor the supernatural experiences people are having, and to try to understand the nature of them.

Their research has uncovered some really interesting things!

HIGH-SCHOOL STUDENTS

In a survey[3] involving four high schools, senior students were asked if they had ever sensed a presence, whether they attributed it to 'God' or not, outside of their physical realm.

Do you know how many of these young people said yes? Around **90%** of them!

Similar results have been replicated by many other universities[4], and research published by the University of Warwick suggests the vast majority of today's youth support a belief in the supernatural, despite being raised in a largely secularised society.

This growing 'awareness of a spiritual dimension' isn't just limited to youth, and many adults are also becoming more aware of the spiritual realm.

---

[3] Paul McQuillian, The 'limit' experience of senior high school students : a study across four Catholic high schools. PhD Thesis, Fitzroy Vic, Australian Catholic University, 2001.

[4] (a) David Hay, The spirituality of adults in Britain, Scottish Journal of Healthcare Chaplaincy, 2002. (b) Kate Adams, God talks to me in my dreams: the occurrence and significance of children's dreams about God, International Journal of Children's Spirituality, 2001. (c) Christian Research Association, "Comparison of Church Attendance Trends in the UK and Australia," *Pointers* 10.1 (2000): 4-5.

LIFE AFTER DEATH

In 2000, a MORI poll, commissioned by the Heaven on Earth show, surveyed members of the UK's public to see how many of them believed in 'Life after Death'.
Some **35%** of respondents said they did.

In 2004, the Daily Telegraph commissioned a similar survey[5], posing the same question. This time, **43%** of people surveyed said 'yes'.

In 2008, Theos Darwin[6] repeated the experiment, and on this occasion, the number of positive responses had risen to **70%**!

Incredible! In just eight years, the proportion of people in the UK who said they believed in 'life after death' doubled, (rising from 35% to 70%), representing an increase of 22 million people!

Despite moves to steer us towards an increasingly secularised state, it would appear that an even greater spiritual awakening is occurring... one which is baffling scientists and academics.

> In just 8 years, an additional 22 million people now believe in 'life after death'!

The phenomenon reminds me of a scene from the science fiction movie, 'Jurassic Park'. The story's plot describes how a

---

[5] By YouGov.
[6] Think tank set up by the Archbishop of Canterbury, Dr Rowan Williams, in 2006. This survey was completed by ComRes.

billionaire philanthropist funded a team of genetic scientists to recreate a population of dinosaurs in a remote tropical island.

In an attempt to control population numbers, the scientists only released female creatures into the enclosures. However, to their shock (and horror) they later discovered a nest of hatched dinosaur eggs and realised that despite their efforts to control the environment, "life found a way" and the creatures had been multiplying.

Whilst the above plot is entirely fictional, the scientist's thwarted efforts to control 'life' provides a poignant parallel with today's society. And despite moves towards increased secularisation, 'life has found a way' and more and more people (including those who have no church, or religious background) are being spiritually awakened.

> Life has
> found a way!

DEEP AND WIDE

The result of this spiritual awakening can be seen across the whole of society.

MOVIES

Pause for a moment and see if you can recall the titles of any recent movies released in the cinema which have a spiritual dimension. Some recent ones include:

> *The Twilight Saga, The Hobbit, The Apparition, ParaNorman, Rise of the Guardians, Brave, Harry Potter, The Medium and Bewitched.*

Block buster movies, like the ones I've just mentioned, cost many millions of pounds (or dollars) to make. For instance the estimated cost of making The Hobbit was $300 million, whilst the cost of making the Harry Potter films was thought to be around $1.1 billion.

Film producers only invest such vast sums of money into their films if they expect there to be a huge audience for them. In the case of the Harry Potter movies, the profit generated (to date) currently stands at more than $6.5 billion, illustrating the hunger amongst ordinary people for supernatural adventures.

ARTS & MEDIA

Similarly, if you walk into a book store, you'll find many of the shelves stacked with best sellers with a spiritual overtone. Best-selling adult books include supernatural thrillers and romances, and some of the most popular children's books include:

> *J K Rowling's Harry Potter novels, which tell about the adventures of a young wizard; Rick Riordan's 'Percy Jackson' series on 'demi-gods'; the Narnia Chronicles; and Holly Webb's books on fairies, dragons and enchantments.*

In addition, most magazines and newspapers now routinely publish articles on spirituality and alternative health[7].

> Ordinary people are hungry for supernatural adventures.

---

[7] Alternative health definition: a variety of therapeutic or preventative health care practices, such as homeopathy, naturopathy and herbal medicine, that do not follow generally accepted medical methods.

HIGH STREETS AND SHOPPING MALLS
Our high streets and shopping malls are also being infiltrated, and it is not unusual to see holistic health shops, spiritual healers and tarot card readers occupying prime retail positions. There's also been an explosion of prayer rooms and sacred places opening up in our shopping centres, airports, hospitals, universities and places of government.

HEALTH
In 2009, over twelve million people in the UK used some form of complementary health medicine, and spent over £213m[8] in the process. Furthermore, around half of the UK's GPs now provide access to Complementary and Alternative Medicine[9], including acupuncture, hypnotherapy, therapeutic massage and art therapy.

BUSINESS
Many employers endorse holistic health measures (yoga, meditation and stress relief therapies) in the workplace, and most management development programmes

> Even health and business markets have been affected.

routinely include sections on 'relaxation' and 'spiritual intelligence'[10].

[8] Mintel, Complementary Medicines UK, Dec 2009
[9] GPs using Complementary and alternative therapies, Rebecca Wallersteiner, netdoctor.co.uk
[10] Practical application of spiritual intelligence in the workplace, Human Resource Management International Digest, 2006.

RELIGION

In addition, some of the most frequently visited websites (other than social networking and porn) are those concerned with the mystical and with spirituality[6].

New Age fairs (now re-branded as Mind-Body-Spirit fairs[11]) have sprung up in many communities, and thousands of spiritual seekers looking for help and direction, are being attracted to them.

Quite simply, we are living in a time where...

Our society is undergoing a spiritual revolution right before our eyes!

And it's happening at pace!

---

[11] Elizabeth Puttick, The Rise of Mind-Body-Soul Publishing, Journal of Alternative Spiritualties and New Age Studies, 2005.

REVIEW QUESTIONS AND ACTIVATION EXERCISES

1. What evidence is there that spiritual hunger is increasing within society?

2. What impact has this awakening had in the nation?

3. What impact has this awakening had on:
   o Your friends, family or work colleagues; and
   o Your local community?

4. How have they demonstrated their spiritual hunger?

5. Spend time asking the Holy Spirit to show you the Father's heart for the spiritually awakened people within your family, your place of work, and your local community. Write down what He shows you.

6. Ask the Holy Spirit for Kingdom strategies to impact different spheres of influence within your community. Write down what He shows you and use that information to partner with God in prayer for your community.

7. What part does God want you to play in helping to usher His Kingdom into the spheres of influence that He's placed you in? Write down and pray about what He shows you.

Chapter two

WHAT'S DRIVING THIS REVOLUTION?

It would be great if these newly-awakened people found
themselves coming along to our churches. But despite our
emerging spiritual society, church attendance in the UK
continues to fall, and fewer and fewer people are identifying
themselves with institutionalised religion.

So what is causing this revolution, and who, or what, is driving
it?

- Why are people from all ages and backgrounds
  becoming more aware of the spiritual realm?
- Why are ordinary people flocking in their thousands to
  New Age fairs and paying good money to try all sorts
  of alternative forms of spirituality?
- In parallel, why are our churches continuing to
  experience falling numbers?; and
- Why are people identifying less and less with
  institutionalised religion?

Are these things happening because evil is on the increase and the enemy taking over the world, or is there another explanation?

BIBLICAL PROPHECY

To answer these questions, we need to re-wind a bit…

Jesus was crucified over 2000 years ago, yet in the last 100 years it seems that more biblical prophecies about the last days have been fulfilled, than at any other time in history. For instance:

1. The Book of Ezekiel foretold Israel's return to her own land.

    'And I will bring them out from the peoples and gather them from the countries, and will bring them to their own land.' (Ez 34:13)

    On the 14th May, 1948, this prophecy was fulfilled as Israel was declared a sovereign state by an act of the United Nations.

2. Speaking of the last days, the Book of Daniel prophesised that

    'many shall run to and fro, and knowledge shall be increased.' (Dan 12:4)

    It's hard to believe that just a hundred years ago one of the main modes of travel was by horse and cart. Yet in the last century, we've seen incredible advancements in our ability to travel including: fast cars, high-speed trains, supersonic jets and space travel.

Similarly, with the advent of computers, the internet and cellular phones, our ability to receive and assimilate knowledge has increased exponentially.

Over the last 100 years, Daniel's prophecy has been fulfilled as society has witnessed a phenomenal increase in the ability to travel & to accrue knowledge.

3. The Book of Ezekiel also predicted that when Israel returned back to her own land – different nations would team up to attack her (Ez 38).

    Barely a week goes by without some report of this in the news.

4. And in the gospel of Matthew, Jesus said a major sign signifying His return would be the gospel being preached in the whole world.

    We're not far from that now, and it may already have happened. (Matt 24:14)

The stage is being set, creating the scene for some of the most phenomenal days since the very beginning of time.

Speaking of the last days, God also promised that:

- *He will pour out His Spirit on all flesh...*
- *Show wonders in the heavens and on the earth, and*
- *Everyone who calls on the name of the LORD will be saved (Joel 2:28-32).*

> As God pours out His Spirit, people are getting hungry...

As God pours out His Spirit, ordinary men, women and children are becoming spiritually hungry and are looking in all sorts of places to find solutions to the spiritual hunger they feel inside. Unless we point them to Jesus, they will continue to look in the wrong places.

In parallel with this outpouring, God has orchestrated the collision of a number of spiritual forces to make this one of the easiest seasons in history to step out and share God's love with others by bringing them into Holy-Spirit led encounters.

These forces are described in more detail in the next chapter.

REVIEW QUESTIONS AND ACTIVATION EXERCISES

1. What do you think is driving the spiritual revolution we are seeing across society?

2. What implications does that have for you?

3. How can you be involved with people on alternative spiritual paths, and still call out the greatness in them?

4. Is it ever wrong to 'call out the gold[12]' in people's lives?

5. Ask the Holy Spirit to give you God's heart for the people in your spheres of influence (family, work colleagues etc.), and to show you (personally) how you can be an ambassador of heaven for these people. Write down what He shows you, and use that information in your prayer life.

Thank you Holy Spirit for allowing me to live in such incredible days! Thank you that You have called me to help usher in one of the largest moves of God this world has ever seen. Help me to be a good ambassador for You in each of the spheres of influence that You have placed me in.

---

[12] i.e. highlight the positive things God has placed within them.

NOTES

Chapter three

A PERFECT SPIRITUAL STORM

The film 'The Perfect Storm' starring George Clooney and Mark Wahlberg, recalls the story of the sword fishing boat, the Andrea Gail, caught in a killer storm, in the North Atlantic in Oct 1991.

Based on a true story, it describes the collision of three different weather patterns:

1. a low pressure system, driving from West to East, which collided with:

2. a high pressure system driving from North to South.

That collision was enough of a catalyst to cause a massive artic weather storm in the North Atlantic, making the surrounding waters treacherous. Then, the unthinkable happened:

3. Hurricane Grace blew in from the South and collided with that artic storm.

The impact of the collision is shown in Figure 1.

As illustrated, the collision caused a 2000 mile wide whirlpool, *stretching all the way from Jamaica to the coast of Labrador.*

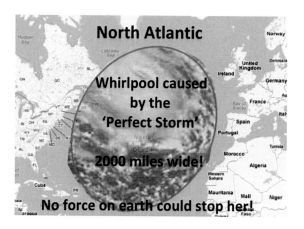

Figure 1: The Perfect Storm

Whenever I re-visit that picture, I can't help noticing how small the size of the UK looks, in comparison to the size of the whirlpool!

Sebastian Junger (who wrote the book the film was based on) stated:

"A mature hurricane is by far the most powerful event in nature. The combined nuclear arsenals of the United States and the former Soviet Union wouldn't contain enough energy to keep a hurricane going for even one day."

I believe our God sometimes releases these colossal, physical manifestations of power to give us just a small glimpse of how big He is (Ps 135:6,7). At times, our perception of Him can be far too small.

However, it's so encouraging to know that the same God who unleashed the incredible, jaw-dropping, force that caused a 2000 mile-wide whirlpool, is the One who lives inside of us!

THE PERFECT SPIRITUAL STORM

The Perfect Storm is an example of a physical phenomenon, caused by three forces of nature colliding. Sometimes, God uses the forces of nature to illustrate something He's unleashing in the spiritual realm[13].

In this current season, God has orchestrated the collision of three spiritual forces to create what can only be described as **The Perfect Spiritual Storm.**

This spiritual storm has implications for the way that we, as followers of Jesus, are able to fulfil the Great Commission and see His Kingdom advanced on the earth.

FORCE ONE
The first of these forces is called the 'Day of the Saints'.

At key points in history, God has released a new revelation of existing truths in scripture, which has led to a fresh understanding of the Church's identity and inheritance.

---

[13] (a) Rom 1:20; (b) Basic Training for the Prophetic Ministry, by Kris Vallotton.

For example:

1520 Protestant Movement

In 1520, Martin Luther received fresh revelation as he was reading from the Book of Romans. As he read

> *'The Just shall live by faith'* (Rom 1:17).

he grasped an understanding that eternal life is a gift, and not something that must (or can) be earned. This revelation led to the birth of the protestant movement.

Prior to this, the church had been buried in dead works and traditions, and existed in a time known as the dark ages.

1900 Pentecostal Movement

In 1900, Charles Parham was reading in the Book of Acts when the Holy Spirit revealed to him that speaking in tongues, is evidence of being baptised in the Spirit. This led to the birth of the Pentecostal movement, and laid the foundation for the Charismatic Movement of the 1960s.

2000 Saints Movement

Today, we're living in a time known as the 'Saint's Movement', where many believers have grasped hold of the words spoken by Jesus, in the Gospel of John:

> *'he who believes in Me, the works that I do he will do also; and greater works than these he will do'* (John 14:12)

The fresh revelation released over that verse is that **all** Christians are called to partner with the Holy Spirit, and see God's Kingdom released on the earth.

The Saint's movement was also spoken of by Daniel:

> *'But the saints of the Most High shall receive the kingdom, and possess the kingdom forever.' (Dan 7:18)*

and coincides with the prophecies given by Joel:

> *'In the last days I will pour out my Spirit on all people. Your sons and daughters will prophecy, your old men will dream dreams, your young men will see visions, even on my servants, both men and women, I will pour out my Spirit' (Joel 2:28,29)*

In summary, we live in a time where ordinary people are called to partner with an awesome God, and see incredible things released on the earth. It marks a shift away from the concept of 'Spiritual Celebrities', where the focus was on the gifting and anointing of individuals such as Billy Graham or Oral Roberts. Instead, today there is a call for each one of us to arise, walk in Kingdom authority, and to represent, or 're-present', Jesus to others through love, signs, wonders and miracles.

Force one is the Saints Movement, where ordinary men, women and children are called to partner with an awesome God to see His signs, wonders and miracles released on the earth.

FORCE TWO

Often when I'm teaching people about prophecy, I ask them if they can give me the names of some famous prophets. Invariably, they cite names like: Elijah, Elisha, Samuel, Jeremiah, and Moses.

And these are good answers. However they are all characters from the Old Testament. As such, they operated under an Old Testament covenant, where they had to wait until the Holy Spirit came upon them, before they could prophecy, or see signs and wonders released on the earth.

Under a New Testament covenant, it's completely different.

As Christians, we've been born again through the Spirit of God. The process of being 'born again' has brought our spirit to life and facilitated on-going communication between the Holy Spirit and our spirit (although we might not always recognise this).

Because we have the Holy Spirit living inside of us, we are in constant communication with Him. Hence, unlike the Old Testament Prophets, we don't need to wait for Him to come upon us to enable us to prophesy, instead we need to learn to **perceive** what the Holy Spirit is saying and learn to discern between His voice and that of our own spirits, or souls.

This means, we don't have to wait for a special moment. We can release God's Kingdom through prophecy, healing and the other spiritual gifts, anytime, anyplace, and anywhere.

When someone comes to us for ministry, whether they are a Christian or not, we can be sure God has thoughts about them. Our job is simply to listen to His heart and share it with them.

> Force two is the revelation that we are called to operate under a New Testament covenant. This means we can partner with the Holy Spirit to see His Kingdom released, anytime, anyplace, anywhere.

FORCE THREE

The third 'force', is where God is putting it on the hearts of His leaders to take the gospel of Jesus outside the church walls and into the everyday meeting places of ordinary people.

Kris Valloton[14] recently gave a prophetic word that confirms this shift of focus. He stated that God was transitioning His Body from being a 'Bethesda Pool' into an 'Ezekiel river'.

So what does that mean?

The pool of Bethesda is mentioned in John 5 (v1-8) and represents a static place where people could come and receive their healing.

In Kris's prophecy, the pool represented the church. Previously the norm was for people to come to the church to receive ministry. In contrast, the river of Ezekiel flowed from the temple and into the everyday meeting places of ordinary people. (Ezekiel 47)

---

[14] A senior leader in Bill Johnson's church in Bethel, California.

The further the river flowed from the temple, the deeper it became. Wherever it flowed, it brought healing and life.

Today, God is releasing a wake-up call to the Church to arise and share the incredible message of the Gospel outside the church walls.

> Force three is the revelation that we are called to take the life-giving message of the Gospel and release the Kingdom of God into the everyday meeting places of ordinary people.

A MASSIVE COLLISION

Today, we live in the most amazing days, where God has orchestrated all three of these forces to come together to create a massive collision in the spiritual realm.

Any one of them on its own is powerful. All three together is like Heaven's equivalent of a nuclear bomb to the power of infinity!

1. We are **all** called to partner with the Holy Spirit and see signs, wonders and miracles released on the earth.
2. We can see this happen: anytime, anyplace, anywhere.
3. We are **all** called to demonstrate the Kingdom of God in the every-day meeting places of ordinary people.

Wow! If you can grasp hold of these truths, and starts walking in the Kingdom power and authority that you are called to walk in, then your home, community and nation(s) will never be the same again!

The spiritually-charged atmosphere generated by the cataclysmic collision of The Perfect Spiritual Storm makes this season one of the most exciting ones in history. It has created a climate where it is easier than it has ever been before, to step out and share God's love with others through love, prophecy, healing, signs, wonders, miracles and other supernatural encounters, and to see ordinary men, women and children brought into life-changing encounters with Jesus.

As an afterthought... did you notice the strapline Wolfgang Petersen (Director) used for the movie of The Perfect Storm?

He stated that:

'No force on earth could stop her...'

I suspect without realising it, Wolfgang was being prophetic! Because we are living in days where God is pouring our His Spirit, causing the political, economic and spiritual landscapes of our world to be impacted, and **'no force on earth can stop Him'**!

REVIEW QUESTIONS AND ACTIVATION EXERCISES

1. What forces are colliding together to create the 'Perfect Spiritual Storm'?
2. What implications do these three forces have for the Church?
3. What implications do these three forces have for you personally?
4. In your own walk with God, what is the most common way He communicates with you?
5. Which gifts do you currently operate in? Write down your answer.
6. How confident are you in operating in these Spiritual gifts?
7. What steps, or additional training, do you need to undertake to improve your confidence and gifting?
8. Make an action plan based on your answer to question 7.
9. Spend time in worship and in the Word. Invite the Holy Spirit to continually fill you, overflow in your life, and to help you bring others into God-encounters.

"Thank you Father for your incredible love, power and glory. Thank you that Your Spirit lives in me, and that I am called to be a supernatural carrier of Your Power and Your Presence. Thank you for the people You have placed around me. Thank you for the plan and purpose You have for their lives. Create a hunger in their hearts for more of You.

Holy Spirit, show me how to share Your Kingdom with them in ways that will help them embrace the destiny You have for them."

Chapter four

CULTURE MATTERS!

The scene has been set. God is continuing to pour out His Spirit on all flesh, causing a spiritual awakening to occur amongst ordinary people in society. He has also orchestrated the perfect conditions for us to step out, share His love with others, and bring people into encounters with His Holy Spirit.

However it's becoming more and more apparent, that some of our traditional ways of sharing the Gospel with people are becoming less and less effective within today's culture.

Despite our emerging spiritual society, **church attendance in the UK continues to fall**, and fewer and fewer people are identifying themselves with institutionalised religion.

Why aren't these newly-awakened seekers turning up at our churches, and why are they not giving Christianity a try?

A Post-Modern Society...

One of the challenges we face is that we live in a post-modern, consumer-based, society, where 'absolutes' are often rejected and 'do-it-yourself' spirituality is not only respected, but fashionable.

Views on
- Right versus wrong; and
- Real versus true

Are determined less now by reason and intellect, and instead, driven by something else...
something successful companies have capitalised on in their advertising campaigns.

> DIY Spirituality has become fashionable

Try completing the following marketing slogans, answering the questions that follow, and see if you can figure out what that 'something' is.

How well do you know these slogans?

---

1. A diamond is... (fill in the blank)

What do you think De Beers, who created that slogan, were selling?

2. Have a break, have a.................................(fill in the blank)

What were Nestle inviting people to do when they purchased this piece of confectionary?

3. Made to make your mouth...........................(fill in the blank)

What were the Wrigley company advertising with this slogan?

4. You know when you've been ....(fill in the blank)

What was Britvic selling with this concept?

Answers are provided at the end of this chapter.

THE COMMON THEME...?

Can you guess what all of these, and other good marketing themes, have in common?

Rather than just give information about a product (or service) they invite people to embark on an **experience.** This approach taps into the psyche of today's society.

In a post-modern society, views on 'right versus wrong', and 'real versus true' are predominately driven by a person's experience, rather than by logic or reason. A key factor behind many decisions is:

"Did it feel good?"

Now I'm not saying that's the correct way of making decisions. Neither am I saying that all decisions are made that way, but **postmodern people are more likely to come to faith through experience** which leads to an understanding of doctrine, **than through prior intellectual assent.**

So if we want to reach today's society effectively with the Gospel, we also need to bring them into experiential encounters.

> People in today's society are looking for 'experiential encounters'.

Actually when you think about it, this isn't a new concept... it's exactly what Jesus did. He continually brought people into life-changing encounters through the Holy Spirit.

ENCOUNTERING JESUS

The gospels are packed full of examples where Jesus demonstrated the Kingdom of God by healing people or by sharing words of knowledge or revelation with them, and then explaining how their encounter linked in with Kingdom principles.

For example, in Luke 4 (v40-43) we read that Jesus laid hands on everyone and healed them. Then he said '*I must preach the Kingdom of God to the other cities also*', implying that 'preaching the Kingdom of God' was as much about bringing people into experiential encounters, as it was about sharing the Word with them.

SIMON PETER

In Luke 5, Jesus encourages Simon Peter to re-cast his net, which results in a miraculous catch of fish. Then He tells Simon that from then on, he will be a *'fisher of men'*.

BLIND BARTIMAEUS

Similarly, in Luke 18 (v35-43), Jesus heals blind Bartimaeus whilst simultaneously explaining the connection between 'healing' and 'faith'.

As well as combining the Word and the Spirit, Jesus also ministered to different people in different ways, depending on what their needs were.

LOVE MATTERS!

THE WOMAN AT THE WELL

For example, Jesus brought the 'woman at the well' (John 4) into a life-changing encounter by releasing words of knowledge to her.

By informing her that He knew her background (i.e. she'd had several previous husbands and was currently living in a sinful relationship), and yet still offering her salvation, He was addressing the very guilt and shame that could have caused her to disqualify herself from ever seeking a saving relationship with Him.

THE LEPER

When Jesus healed the leper (Mark 1:40-45), He used a different approach.

In biblical times, if you caught leprosy, you faced the inevitable prospect of a slow and painful death. There was no known cure, and the disease would relentlessly damage your skin, nerves and limbs.

At the initial stages of infection, people would sometimes be able to cover up the outward effects of the disease, however it was only be a matter of time before it would become apparent to others. Once people realised someone had leprosy, they were ostracised and separated from the rest of society.

For a leper, catching the disease and facing a slow, painful, death was horrendous enough, but being rejected and cut-off by everyone you knew and loved as well, must have been unbearable. Under Jewish law, anyone who came into contact with a leper was also classified as 'unclean'.

So, when we read the account of Jesus healing the leper in Mark's Gospel, the approach He took was breath-taking. In verse 41 we read,

*'then Jesus, moved with compassion, stretched out His hand and **touched him**... as soon as He had spoken, immediately the leprosy left him and he was healed.'*

> Jesus 'brought' the Kingdom, and 'taught' the Kingdom'.

By getting up close and personal, and deliberately reaching out His hand to touch him in full view of everybody, Jesus cut across the religious and judgemental barriers of the culture. By doing so, He would undoubtedly have caused people to feel shocked and offended.

Why did Jesus take this approach? Because…

> Jesus knew what 'love looked like'.

Jesus could have healed the leper simply by speaking to the disease and rebuking it. But by stretching out His hand and touching him, Jesus not only healed his physical condition, but met a deep-seated need for physical contact. Through the power of touch, He helped restore the man's dignity, honour and self-respect.

Similarly, by offering salvation to the woman at the well (despite her sinful background), He was letting her know that she was valued and loved, irrespective of the decisions and choices she had made in the past. That reassurance was exactly what she needed to hear.

In these two examples, Jesus demonstrated a principle we need to embrace if we want to reach today's society with the life-saving message of the Gospel.

> Jesus looked to see what 'love looked like' for the people He wanted to reach, and then He brought them into a life-changing encounter by addressing that need.

We need to do the same.

Leprosy might not be a prevalent issue in Western society, but there are many other things that people can go through that can leave them feeling ashamed, rejected, cut-off, or not good enough.

GEMMA'S STORY

Gemma came to one of our gazebo-style outreaches in Glasgow last winter. It was one of the coldest weather spells we'd had in years and we were absolutely freezing! Despite the artic conditions, Gemma came to our stall. She worked as a prostitute and had just finished her shift. Still in her 'working clothes' she sat down. Her face looked hard, reflecting years of disappointment, rejection and judgement.

> *"Come on then, let's see what you've got… I could do with a laugh!"*

As I looked at her, I felt an unbelievable surge of the Father's love. I looked straight into her angry, hard eyes, took hold of her hands and released God's words of value and hope into her. As I spoke, the Holy Spirit revealed some of the dreams she'd had as a little girl, and let her know He'd not forgotten them. He told her how he'd been with her through all of her toughest times, and how His heart broke for her pain.

Within minutes, both of us were in tears. And as we sat there, our amazing God released wave upon wave of His love over her. Gemma couldn't wait to start a saving relationship with Jesus and asked Him into her life, right in the middle of a busy street, in the middle of winter.

For Gemma, '*love looked like*' a simple touch, combined with the Father's love.

GOD DOESN'T DO UGLY!

Having leprosy would have caused the leper to look disfigured, and he was probably ashamed of his appearance. Today, there might not be many people in our society with leprosy, but there are lots of people who wish they looked a bit different.

A survey issued by Social Issues Research Centre[15] discovered that eight out of ten teenage girls in the UK are unhappy with their appearance.

Human infants begin to recognise themselves in mirrors when they are around two and a half years old. Research suggests that female humans begin to dislike what they see just two years later!

No wonder satan's called the father of lies!

Aimee came along to one of our outreach events in an impoverished part of Glasgow. As she sat down I asked the Holy Spirit for something that would really impact her. I was expecting something profound, but all I sensed Him say was "tell her she's beautiful". As I shared that word with her she started to cry and said:

"No I'm not, I'm ugly."

Then I felt the Holy Spirit prompt me to tell her:

"God wants you to know He doesn't do 'ugly'! Do you know why He made you? He wanted one, didn't have

---

[15] Survey amongst teenage girls, Social Issues Research Centre, Kate Fox 1997

one, and so He made one! And He says you're beautiful!"

Aimee was just seventeen years old, and had spent most of her life believing she was ugly and that she'd been an 'accident'. She came to us with no self-worth, but as the Father showed her His love, the lies that had encaged her were broken. Bit by bit, He restored her sense of value and worth.

For Aimee, *'love looked like'* unconditional love, reassurance and affirmation.

> Take time to see what 'love looks like' for the people you're trying to reach.

LANGUAGE MATTERS!

In addition to recognising what *'love looked like'*, Jesus also spoke the language of His day using parables and metaphors people could understand and easily relate to.

Similarly, Paul urged the early church to think carefully about how they communicated with 'not-yet' believers, and to make every effort to explain the gospel to them in ways that were culturally relevant.

> Jesus spoke the language of the people.

'If you talk to people in a language they don't understand, how will they know what you mean? You might as well be talking to an empty room.
(1 Cor 14:9-11).

> Paul urged believers to be culturally relevant.

'To the Jews I become like a Jew, to win the Jews. To those under the law I become like one under the law... so as to win those under the law... I become all things to all men so that by all possible means I might save some.' (1 Cor 9:20-23)

To reach our generation of spiritual seekers, we need to do likewise. People are often very open to talking about God (and encountering Him) when we speak to them in a language they can understand.

At our outreach events, we've found that when we use the language of the people we're trying to reach, they are much more likely to come for ministry.

Despite Scotland being a small country, we've noticed language differences between people who live in different parts of the country, and amongst those who operate in different spheres of influence.

One example is the term 'prophecy'. Most people with a church background are familiar (and comfortable) with that term. However, the word 'prophecy' is not well understood by 'un-churched' people, particularly those who have a background in alternative spirituality. Many of these people would describe our description of 'prophecy' as a *spiritual reading* from the Spirit of Jesus.

When trying to engage with people from that background, we therefore use the phrase 'spiritual reading' and explain that we are going to ask the Spirit of Jesus if He has anything He'd like us to share with them.

Similarly, we've found that many people from a business or corporate background prefer the term 'destiny word' rather than 'prophecy' or 'spiritual reading'. Thus we will use the phrase 'destiny word' if we are ministering to people within that context.

Over the years, as our outreach teams have spent time with seekers from all different backgrounds, we've become familiar with many of the terms and phrases they use. I've included a glossary of common terms and phrases in Appendix 1, along with a list of the different names of God in Appendix 2.

> Make an effort to learn the language of the people you are trying to reach.

BRINGING PEOPLE INTO ENCOUNTERS

In the previous sections, I've looked at keys Jesus used to bring people into experiential life-changing encounters. These included:

1. Combining the Word and the Spirit, by bringing people into an encounter and then linking their experience back to God's character and to scripture.
2. Recognising 'what love looked like' for the people He wanted to reach.
3. Speaking to people in a language they could understand.

There's another key that will help us bring people into encounters with the Holy Spirit…

HEAVEN'S RHYTHM

Often when I'm teaching on supernatural evangelism, I'll ask people the following question:

> *"Can anyone tell me, how do you breathe?*

Often, I'm met with a sea of confused expressions! But it's not a trick question! How do you breathe?

God has created you to breathe by taking a breath, and then releasing a breath. When He designed you, He created some rhythms (or patterns) for you to live by. Breathing is one of those rhythms. You breathe in, you breathe out. You receive, you release.

What would happen if you tried breathing out continuously?

You'd probably look a bit weird! You might go red in the face, become light-headed, and fall over. Feel free to try this one at home!

The point is:

Life has a Rhythm.

And some of these rhythms apply in the supernatural realm too.

You can't give out what you haven't received!

- If you want to release God's love to others, you've got to receive it first;
- If you want to release a fresh anointing for signs, wonders and miracles, you have to be freshly anointed; and
- If you want to bring people into encounters with God, you need to make sure you're having regular encounters with Him.

Often before our outreach events, we'll spend time in worship, saturating in God's Presence - being filled up with His love, Presence, and Power. Having our spiritual eyes recalibrated, so we see things from Heaven's perspective. Reminding ourselves of how incredible our God is, and that nothing is impossible with Him.

Scripture tells us: We love God, because He first loved us (1 John 4:19), and urges us to be continually filled with the Holy Spirit (Eph 5:18, Acts 13:52).

A fourth key is:

> Have an encounter, and then become an encounter.

Answers to the 'slogan' quiz.

---

1. **A diamond is…. [forever]**

   De Beers were not just selling gemstones , but they selling the idea of lasting love.

2. **Have a break, have a… [Kit Kat]**

   Nestle weren't just encouraging people to buy a chocolate bar, but inviting people to embark a break from the stress of life, to relax and unwind, to take time out.

3. **Made to make your mouth… [water]**

   Rather than just selling a sweet, the Wrigley Company were selling the experience of making your mouth water.

4. **You know when you've been tango'd**

   Britvic were selling the concept of having a good time.

REVIEW QUESTIONS AND ACTIVATION EXERCISES

1. Within a post-modern, consumer-based, society, what key factor lies behind many personal decisions that people make?

2. How did Jesus demonstrate the Kingdom of God to people?

3. Fill in the blanks...
   a. Jesus combined the Word and the _____ in His ministry.

   b. Jesus knew what _____ looked like for the people He wanted to reach.

   c. Jesus spoke the _____ of His day.

4. How should we demonstrate God's Kingdom to people?

5. How can you absorb and utilise these truths into your own supernatural walk with God? Write down your answer.

   "Father, thank you for Jesus. Thank you that by His sacrifice on the cross, He made it possible for me to enjoy an incredible friendship with You. Holy Spirit, show me how to use the keys, Jesus gave us for releasing the reality of the Kingdom of God to the people around me. Help me to combine the truths of the Word with Your Holy Spirit, to understand 'what love looks like' for them, and to be able to communicate with them in a language they understand."

Chapter five

GOOD CHRISTIANS DON'T DO THAT, DO THEY…?

Some years ago, I received an invitation that changed the way I viewed spiritual seekers and altered the approach I took to evangelism.

I was invited to help out at a Healing Rooms[16] outreach into a 'Body and Soul' fair.

At first, I wasn't too sure about going. I come from an Evangelical / Baptist background, and I didn't think 'good' Christians should be seen near these places, let alone attend them. So I gave a 'good' Christian response and said "*let me pray about it*", fully expecting that to be the end of it.

However, as I prayed, I felt a clear prompting from the Holy Spirit. The more I prayed, the more I felt I needed to go. I had a sense God wanted to show me something.

However, I was concerned that something in the atmosphere might 'contaminate' me, so I arranged for an army of

---

[16] Healing Rooms is an international ministry that offers free healing prayer (based on biblical principles) to members of the public.

intercessors to pray for me, before, during and afterwards, and went along fully expecting the place to be full of 'weirdos', and people on the fringe of society!

> I thought I might get contaminated!

We were allocated a space for our stall in the corner of the building, right next to some Reiki healers, spiritualists and tarot card readers. We put up signs offering free Christian prayer, and waited to see what would happen.

I couldn't believe the response we received. Before long, our stall became one of the busiest in the place, and over that one weekend, our little team of about 6 volunteers prayed for over 90 people.

> 12 people accepted salvation!

Twelve of these precious people went on to accept the offer of salvation through Jesus and embarked on the beginning of a life-changing journey of friendship with God. Other people experienced physical healing, and many were visibly impacted as they encountered the unconditional love of Jesus.

Perhaps the thing that surprised me most of all, was the people who attended were ordinary folk: mums, dads, grannies, granddads and young people. They were not 'weird' or 'strange', but ordinary people, who had become spiritually hungry, and were simply looking for answers to the spiritual void they felt inside.

> Most attendees were ordinary people who'd simply become spiritually hungry.

Their quest led many of them to attend New Age spiritual fairs in their thousands.

For many years, I'd tried all sorts of evangelistic methods in my attempt to share the gospel with others, including: open-air meetings, distributing gospel tracts, door-to-door visits, evangelistic sketches, and many more alternatives. Yet the fruit we experienced in that weekend was breath-taking. And the approach taken was so simple and unobtrusive.

We simply invited people to come and experience the healing power and presence of Jesus, and as they did so, they were overwhelmed by His love.

The experience left me stunned.

WHAT ARE TODAY'S SEEKERS LOOKING FOR?

So what kind of experience, are today's seekers looking for?

Just as in Biblical days, there is no 'one size fit's all', and they're looking for different things including:

1. Healing;
2. Guidance;
3. Comfort;
4. Peace; and
5. Love & acceptance

In an attempt to fulfil these needs, many searching for physical or emotional healing have embraced spiritual alternatives like

Reiki, whilst those seeking guidance or comfort have sought solutions through spiritualism or angel guides.

Similarly those looking for peace have considered alternatives like yoga, whilst others have simply wanted to be part of a community where they could feel accepted, and explore their new-found spirituality without criticism or judgment.

> All of the things spiritual seekers are looking for can be found through relationship with Jesus Christ.

THE GAP

Unfortunately many seekers have a perception of the Church as a hierarchical, man-made, institution girded by rigid rules and regulations. Many view it as 'religious' rather than 'spiritual', and 'intellectual' rather than 'emotional'[17].

For a spiritually awakened, post-modern, person, this perception is the polar opposite of what they are searching for.

> Spiritual seekers are not interested in religion!

Yet, true Christian spirituality has little to do with stuffy rules and regulations, and everything to do with passionate, untamed, outrageous love.

Choosing to be a follower of Jesus is about entering an authentic, dynamic, relationship with an incredible God, who

---

[17] Many churches do of course offer people a spiritual experience! However a lot of people don't recognise this.

so passionately desires friendship with us, that He bore the ultimate sacrifice to make friendship not only possible, but utterly accessible.

In our efforts to share God's love with others, we need to give them a glimpse of what true Christian spirituality is, i.e. Christianity beyond religion.

> Christianity is about having an authentic friendship with an incredible God.

Perhaps not surprisingly, we've found that when many of these seekers are brought into face-to-face, encounters with the Living God, their alternative forms of spirituality appear empty and hollow by comparison.

Once they 'taste' of God's love, many are irrevocably smitten, and become eager to embark on a journey of friendship with Him, and leave their former practices behind.

TASTER SESSIONS

At our outreach events, we apply a Presence-led, evangelistic model, where people are invited to have a 'free spiritual encounter' with the Spirit of Jesus (i.e. the Holy Spirit).

> Once seekers 'taste' God's love, they become irrevocably smitten.

Afterwards, we provide opportunities to ask questions and discuss what they experienced.

To encourage as many people as possible to encounter Jesus, we offer a range of Christian ministry options to address the various 'love languages' and needs people have. These include:

- **Spiritual healing**, for physical, emotional & spiritual conditions; and
- **Prophecy**, for direction & guidance;
- **Head, shoulder and hand massage** combined with prayer, for those who need 'stress-relief' and whose love language is touch;
- **Spiritual art** for people who are more likely to be impacted visually than audibly. (Here our artists simply pray and ask God if there's a sketch or picture they can quickly draw which will help them share God's love with their visitor.);
- **Dream interpretation** using biblical principles, to help them discern what (if anything) God might be saying to them through their dreams.
- **De-stressing meditation** seminars and exercises, using scriptures, biblical truths and Christian meditation music.
- **Live music** by Christian artists, to help host an atmosphere of worship.

We've also partnered with many churches and other organisations to hold community fun days where we've provided a range of family-friendly activities alongside different ministry options. These have included: bouncy castles, face-painting, balloon sculpting and other activities.

DOES IT WORK?

As we've applied this approach, we've seen thousands of people flock to our outreach events, and hundreds brought into a saving relationship with Jesus. We've also seen the Holy Spirit do some incredible miracles.

As people have encountered Jesus, many of them have told us they've been healed from:

- deafness;
- arthritis;
- back pain;
- knee injuries;
- broken bones;
- depression;
- fibromyalgia;
- migraines; and
- many more conditions.

I've included some of their stories below...

JOE

'Joe' was a homeless man who came along to an event in Glasgow. Some years ago, he fell from a bridge, smashing his hip and leg. He had to have steel plates inserted, to strengthen his leg, which left him unable to bend it properly.

Initially, Joe came across as 'tough' and sceptical, but as the team prayed, God's Presence tangibly fell, and unprompted, he stood to his feet and started testing his injury.

Seconds later he bent down and did squat thrusts on the floor!
His face was beaming as he exclaimed: *"I didnae believe in all
this stuff, but I dae now!"*

A few moments later Joe asked to enter into a saving
relationship with Jesus.

Joe came to Jesus through a healing encounter

JENNY

'Jenny', was a teenager who came to an outreach in Edinburgh
at the start of the summer. You could tell by her demeanour
that she'd seen and experienced things, no person should ever
have to see or experience. She'd been abused and raped as a
young girl, and the trauma had left her with no confidence or
self-worth. Watching her stare at the carpet as she spoke was
painful.

'Ellie', had become a Christian just a few months earlier, and
she offered to pray with Jenny. As Ellie invited Father God to
pour His love into this precious, broken, girl, a beautiful
miracle took place...

Wave upon wave of His love swept over her. She was
completely overwhelmed, and for the first time in her life, felt
loved, valued and accepted. Moments later, she lifted her tear-
stained face and said, *"I feel like a new person...!"*

When Jenny encountered Father God, she received emotional healing.

YOUNG PEOPLE

Over the last few years we've seen an increasing spiritual awakening happening amongst young people and students. Just before Christmas, we held an outreach at a large spiritual fair in Glasgow.

We were incredibly busy, but noticed a marked increase in the number of youths who came along. They came in groups of four and five at a time, looking for spiritual direction. All of them had unforgettable, life-changing, encounters and several received salvation.

> Many young people received salvation as they encountered the revelatory gifts of the Holy Spirit.

PEOPLE FROM DIFFERENT FAITHS

We've also noticed an increasing number of people coming along from different faiths and backgrounds, and many Hindus, Muslims and Spiritualists have found salvation after having an experiential encounter with Jesus.

Some of them have even encountered God through their dreams. Last summer, we held a 'gazebo-style' outreach in St Andrews, and a Muslim lady, 'A'ida', came along to have her dream interpreted. Part of the interpretation required her to talk to Jesus.

She was taken aback and asked…

"Can someone like me talk to the great prophet Jesus?"

We encouraged her to close her eyes, start the dialogue and see what happened. Within moments she was fully engaged in an intimate conversation with the King of kings. A few minutes later, A'ida left, beaming, with the life-changing revelation that she could talk to our amazing Jesus anytime, any place…

A'ida had an encounter with Jesus through dream interpretation.

Not 'One-Off' Isolated Incidents

These stories are not 'one-off', isolated incidents. We've seen hundreds of people enter a saving relationship with Jesus after experiencing something of His love, grace, power and presence.

In Conclusion…

Our God is creating a spiritual hunger in the hearts of His lost children. As they become spiritually awakened, they are searching for solutions to the spiritual void they feel.

Everything they are looking for can be found in Jesus Christ, but unless we find ways of helping them experience Him, they will continue to look elsewhere for answers.

REVIEW QUESTIONS AND ACTIVATION EXERCISES

1. What kind of things are many of today's spiritual seekers looking for?

2. How do many people in society view the Church?

3. What is true Christian spirituality?

4. What does it mean to be a follower of Jesus?

5. How can we bridge the gap between people's perceptions of Christianity and the reality of life in Jesus? Write down your answer.

6. Ask the Holy Spirit for a personal strategy for bringing people into life-changing encounters with Jesus. Write down what He shows you.

7. Go on some Kingdom sharing encounters with God! One possibility for doing this is to join one of our Light and Life outreach teams and experience first-hand what it's like to see people brought into Presence-based encounters with the Living God.

8. Start a journal to record the supernatural adventures God takes you on.

Chapter six

BUILDING BRIDGES

As you read through the previous chapters, I hope you got a feel for the size of the spiritual revolution that is taking place.

I used to consider the phrase 'spiritual seeker' as referring to a small minority group on the edge of society. But that definition is wrong. As God continues to pour out His Spirit, the majority of ordinary people are experiencing a spiritual awakening. The effects of which, are ricocheting across every sphere of society, and transcending all cultures, age groups and backgrounds.

This 'awakening' is particularly prevalent amongst young people and the under-forties (i.e. those born in the 70s and afterwards).

A recent survey[18] revealed that three out of every four teenagers, have engaged in at least one type of psychic or witchcraft-related activity, including: using Ouija boards; reading books about witchcraft or New Age-related activity, playing computer games involving sorcery or witchcraft, and having their fortune told.

---

[18] "New Research Explores Teenage Views and Behaviour Regarding the Supernatural," Barna Update, January 23, 2006.

> The phrase 'spiritual seeker' refers to most of the people we come into contact with.

Many of these 'awakened' people are not 'seasoned practitioners', but curious individuals who have tried a range of spiritual alternatives in an attempt to quench the spiritual thirst they feel.

And because we live in a post-modern, consumer-based society, most have adopted a 'do-it-yourself' ethos to their spirituality which results in a synchronistic, 'pick and mix', attitude to different practices, depending on their hunger and preferences.

For instance, people with angel guides may also frequent Reiki practitioners, and people will actively 'shop around' between psychics, clairvoyants, and tarot card readers for the 'best deal' on 'supernatural guidance'.

If we are to fulfil our God-given commission of 'making disciples of all nations' (Matt 28), we need to find ways of encouraging these spiritually awakened seekers to have life-changing encounters with Jesus.

In the sections that follow, I look at some of the most common spiritual alternatives people are likely to have encountered and provide guidelines for helping people with exposure to these practices encounter Jesus – irrespective of whether they are seasoned practitioners, or people who occasionally dabble with those alternative forms of spirituality.

When attempting to build a bridge with those people, it is important to:

1. Try to understand what 'love' looks like for the person you're trying to reach;
2. Treat them like valued individuals, and show them love, honour and respect;
3. Listen to what they have to say, and learn to speak (at least some of) their language;
4. Build trust; and
5. Invite them to have a power encounter with Jesus.

ANGELS AND ANGEL GUIDES

AN OVERVIEW
Many people today have a fascination with angels and angel guides.

New Age teaching on angels states that:

1) they are 'beings of light' from the '7th dimension (or higher)';
2) to connect with angels effectively, seekers should become a spiritual medium or clairvoyant; and
3) angels communicate with humans 'telepathically'.

It also teaches that angels fall into different classifications including:

Guardian angels: believed to be assigned to us at birth. Their 'purpose' includes protecting people and guiding them towards the 'divine blueprint' for their life (which individuals are supposed to have 'agreed to before they were born');

Archangels: believed to be a 'higher order' of angels whose role it is to direct and oversee the actions of other angels.

Different archangels are thought to have different gifts, skills and abilities, which include: ruling over geographical regions, and having oversight of specific tasks including: protecting people and places; helping people to 'see' into the spiritual realm; guiding; healing and purifying people and places.

Other angels: that can be called upon to help seekers: prosper; forge better relationships; obtain favour and influence; and achieve success in other areas.

CONCERNS

From a biblical perspective there are many concerns over New Age teaching on angels. As mentioned, to communicate with these 'angels', spiritual seekers are encouraged to practice clairvoyance or mediumship, both of which are strictly forbidden by scripture.

> *Let no one be found among you who sacrifices their son or daughter in the fire, who practises divination or sorcery, interprets omens, engages in witchcraft, or*

casts spells, or who is a medium or spiritist or who consults the dead.(Deut 18:10,11)

Seekers are taught that 'angels' are responsible for 'purifying us', guiding us, healing us, and much more. However as Christians we know it is the sanctifying blood of Christ that purifies us, and the Holy Spirit who guides us.

> By attributing these functions to 'angels', New Age teaching is turning people away from the true Godhead.

Thus the angels that many seekers 'connect' with are from satan, and not from God.

Scripture tells us that satan's mission is to *'steal, kill and destroy'* humanity (John 10:10), and therefore, it is not surprising, that many seekers who engage with such 'angels' experience nightmares, ill health, paranoia, schizophrenia, depression, and other forms of mental illness.

So, how can we help these people encounter Jesus?

STEP ONE: BUILD A BRIDGE
The first step is to build a bridge, and then encourage them to encounter Jesus for themselves.

One way of building a bridge with someone who has an angel guide (or would like one), is to let them know that one of the names of Jesus is the **God of the Angel Army**.

The phrase Lord God of Hosts, literally means Lord God of the angels and other heavenly beings. In The Message bible, Peterson routinely translates this phrase as 'the God of the angel army' (Zec 8:1, 4; Mal 3:1, 5; Is 48:2).

When someone talks to me about their angel guide (or their desire to have one) I usually respond by listening to what they have to say, inform them that one of the names of Jesus is the 'God of the angel army', and let them know that He often sends angels to minister to us too.

During the conversation, I'll look for an opportunity to explain there are good and bad angels in existence. Many people recognise this, and agree they don't want 'bad' angels having any influence over their life. This provides an opportunity to offer to pray with them and 'close down' the influence of angels (or other spiritual entities) that are not from a 'true and good' source (i.e. Jesus). We can also encourage them to **let Jesus be the One who chooses which angel** (if any) should minister to them in the future.

Often, after praying this type of prayer, most seekers sense a difference in the atmosphere around them and feel much 'lighter' and 'freer'. At this point, they become much more receptive to hearing the message of the Gospel.

DIALOGUE
The following table illustrates a typical dialogue I would have with someone who has angel guides.

Sample dialogue: seeker with an angel guide

Me:	*"so you have an angel guide?"*
Seeker:	*"yes"*
Me:	*"we sometimes have angels help us out too. In fact, one of the names of our God is 'the God of the angel army"*
Seeker:	*"really?"*
Me:	*"Yes, He often sends angels to help His followers. But did you know there are good angels and bad angels?"*
Seeker:	*"Yeah, I'd heard that…"*
Me:	*"I've met quite a few people who had bad angels…"*
Seeker:	*"Really? What was that like?"*
Me:	*"Well, to begin with, they seemed okay. But then the person would sometimes feel scared, or would just sense a 'bad presence' around them. In some cases, they might experience nightmares or feel a bit depressed. Bad angels often try to trick people into letting them hang around them, then they can turn nasty and become a pest"*
Seeker:	*"that sounds awful…"*

Me: *"Yes, it can be. The problem is, it can be difficult for people to know what kind of angel they've got, at least to begin with. Then if they find out they've got a bad one, most folk don't know what to do about it, but that's something we can help with."*

Seeker: *"how can you help?"*

Me: *"we can offer 'spiritual cleansing', where we pray for any negative influence that's affecting someone to be removed. Then we forbid any angel that's not from a 'good and true source[19]' from influencing that person in the future.*

It's really simple and only takes a few minutes. Whenever we've helped people that way, they've felt so much better afterwards.

The only angels that leave are 'bad' ones, and no one wants them influencing their lives anyway."

Pause… let the implications of what you've just said sink in for a moment or two, then you can ask…

"Would you like us to pray that any negative influence you might have picked up along the way would be removed…?"

---

[19] i.e. Jesus

Over the years, as we've ministered to people with angel guides, we've rarely come across anyone who wasn't open to receiving 'cleansing prayer'.

Many people seeking angel guides are simply looking for comfort or direction. This fact can also help us build a bridge with them, because another name for our amazing God is '**The God of all Comfort**' (2 Cor 1:3), and throughout scripture, the Holy Spirit is referred to as our **Guide** and our **Comforter**.

STEP TWO: LET THEM ENCOUNTER JESUS

The second step, after building a bridge, is to let them encounter Jesus.

If the person is open to discussion, you can ask them some exploratory questions…

> *"What was it that drew you to angels?"*
> *"How did you become interested in angels?"*

Depending on their response, you can ask them if they've tried going directly to the 'God of all Comfort', or whether they've experienced the Holy Spirit's ability to provide guidance. If they're willing to encounter the Holy Spirit, simply invite Him to come and fill them with His Peace, or ask the Holy Spirit to give you a word of comfort, guidance or direction for them.

Normally, when someone with an angel guide encounters God's peace, it far exceeds anything they've experienced from their 'angel'. Which is hardly surprising, given that satan can only generate a poor counterfeit of the peace that Jesus brings. Many have responded by saying:

"That was incredible; I've never felt peace like that before..."

Similarly, when you ask the Holy Spirit for words of knowledge, or prophetic words for them, the revelation He brings will resonate much more with their spirit than any 'guidance' they've ever received from an 'angel'. When God speaks, His words carry a richness, depth and authority not found amongst the alternative forms of spiritualty.

It is not uncommon for people to respond to the revelation released by the Holy Spirit by saying:

> *"that was so accurate! I've just paid £40 to have my cards read, and this was so much better, and it was free... this is just amazing!"*

Then you can explain…

> *"yes... but it's all about having the right source. The people you've gone to in the past have had their own source, whether it's been an angel or another 'spiritual channel', but our source... the one you've just experienced, is the Spirit of Jesus.*
>
> *Sometimes He's called the Holy Spirit. And the reason it was so accurate is that the Spirit of Jesus knows everything about you. He knew you even before you were born, even when you were in your mother's womb..."*

By engaging with people in this way, you can weave in the truth of scripture in a way that's relevant and helpful, but more importantly, in a way in which they're likely to listen.

Each person is an individual, on their own journey, with their own needs, but our God knows everything about them. As you share the things He gives you, they will not only have an incredible experiences, they will be left hungry for even more encounters with 'the God who Speaks' and who knows them so well.

If appropriate, you can proceed to share the gospel with them (in plain English), leaving space for questions and discussion.

STEP THREE: NEXT STEPS

As you draw your ministry session, to a close, make sure you present some options to help them further along in their journey.

'CHI', 'CHAKRAS' & 'AURA'

AN OVERVIEW

Traditional Chinese medicine asserts 'Chi[20]' to be the 'energy life flow' that flows through all of creation. Practitioners believe it contains both positive (yin) and negative (yang) energy. The 'Chi' surrounding objects and life forms, is referred to as 'aura'.

---

[20] (a) Sometimes referred to as Ki, Qi, or Prana. (b) Belief in 'Chi' is at the foundation of eastern practices including: Yoga, martial arts, Reiki, Feng Shui and Acupressure.

It is taught that humans have seven separate points (chakras) in their bodies through which 'Chi' can be received. Any obstruction, or imbalance, in a person's 'Chi' is thought to cause stress, or ill health, and it is hoped that cleansing a person's 'chakra' will rebalance their 'Chi' and restore them to health. Practitioners attempt to 'cleanse' charkas through: Reiki, Yoga and other practices.

CONCERNS

The belief system surrounding 'Chi', 'chakras' and 'auras' centre on an impersonal 'energy life-force', rather than the true Trinitarian, Living God, or the Person of the Holy Spirit.

Followers are taught that understanding their chakras will help them:

- experience 'fullness of life' through 'self-actualisation';
- obtain 'freedom' from doubt and guilt by balancing their 'Chi'; and
- access 'higher information', or intelligence, from the spirit realm.

However, as Christians we know fullness of life is only obtained through salvation in Jesus Christ.

Teaching people they can obtain personal freedom and fulfilment by balancing their 'Chi', diverts them away from the only true source (i.e. Jesus) who can bring them redemption, forgiveness and cleansing.

In addition, by attempting to engage with 'higher energies' through chakras, practitioners are unwittingly engaging with demonic entities.

So how can we bring people who engage in these practices into an encounter with Jesus?

STEP ONE: BUILD A BRIDGE
Seekers, who believe in these teachings, want to experience what it feels like to be spiritually cleansed, so they can experience a sense of love, peace and wellbeing.

To build a bridge, I would let them know I understood their desire to be cleansed, so they could experience those feelings.

As much as possible, I would use their language and their phraseology. For instance, because they use the phrase 'energy life force', we can tell them that one of the names of Jesus is 'The Life', and that His Spirit is the ultimate 'Life Force'. I would also explain that He has incredible cleansing powers, the highest in the universe and beyond.

STEP TWO: LET THEM ENCOUNTER JESUS
If they are willing, I would offer to pray for them to experience a 'spiritual cleansing', where the influence of any 'energy' not from a true and good source (i.e. not from Jesus) is removed from their life, and for them to experience His love, peace and healing power.

Most people who encounter Jesus in this way are overwhelmed, and become keen to find out more about who He is, and how they can connect with Him on a personal level.

DIALOGUE

The following table illustrates the type of dialogue I might have with a seeker who believes in Chi.

Sample dialogue: seeker who believes in Chi
Me: *"I understand, you need to have a spiritual cleansing, so you can experience a flow of pure life-giving energy, and be filled with love and peace."*
Seeker: *"That's right! I feel so 'heavy'... I think I've been contaminated by 'negative energy'."*
Me: *"We've been trained to offer 'spiritual cleansing. Would you like us to pray for you?"*
Seeker: *"That would be great"*
Me: *"We'd love to.*   *Just so you know, our 'source' is the Spirit of Jesus, so when we pray for you, it's the power of His Spirit you'll experience.*   *One of the names of Jesus is 'the Life', and His Spirit is the ultimate 'Life Force'."*
Seeker: *"I didn't know that..."*

Then simply forbid any spirit, other than the Spirit of Jesus from influencing them, and invite the Spirit of Jesus (i.e. the Holy Spirit) to let them experience His Presence, His love, peace and, if appropriate, healing.

> Me: *"How does that feel?"*
>
> Seeker: *"Amazing, I've never experienced peace*
>   *like it…"*

Depending on how the Holy Spirit leads, it may be possible to share more of the Gospel message with them.

STEP THREE: NEXT STEPS
Don't forget to offer suggestions that will help them explore Christianity further, or to grow in their friendship with Jesus.

REIKI PRACTITIONERS

AN OVERVIEW
One of the most popular methods of alternative spiritual healing is Reiki.

The word Reiki is composed of two Japanese words, Rei and Ki[21], where Rei can be defined as 'ghost' and 'Ki' defined as vapour. Reiki practitioners believe 'Rei' represents the 'Higher Intelligence' that guides and created the universe, whilst 'Ki' is thought to be the 'life force' that 'animates' the physical organs and tissues of all living things.

Reiki practitioners believe sickness is caused by a restriction of 'Ki', caused by negative thoughts or feelings.

---

[21] *Sometimes called Chi, Qi, or Prana.*

Reiki teaching asserts that:
- practitioners can access 'Rei' through 'Reiki guides';
- Reiki guides are spiritual entities that can take different forms including: humanoids, animals, angels, spheres of light, and others; and
- these guides show practitioners how to harness the energy, or 'Rei', from 'the higher intelligence', and how to 'impart' that 'healing energy' to others.

Practitioners believe the 'guide' they work with determines the healing power they can access and release. There is an established 'pecking order' (or hierarchy), where new practitioners are given access to less powerful spirit guides, whilst experienced practitioners are given access to more powerful guides.

The practice of Reiki includes three levels (or degrees) of 'expertise':

First degree practitioners (beginners) are introduced to the concept of spiritual healing, and given a basic understanding of the practice of Reiki.

Second degree practitioners (intermediate) have received some training on spirit guides, i.e. how to contact them, and liaise with them to harness the power of 'Rei'.

Third degree practitioners (advanced) have been taught to give complete control of their being, to another spirit. They believe this enables them to become an efficient channel through which Reiki energy can flow.

CONCERNS

From a Christian perspective, there are many concerns over the practice of Reiki.

> By attributing healing to a 'higher intelligence' (called Rei), practitioners are turning people's attention away from the Living God, whose name is Jehovah Rapha – the God who heals us.

True healing for our body, soul and spirit is found through Jesus, and scripture tells us that it is by His wounds we are healed (Is 53). Healing is part of the atoning work of the cross.

Perhaps even more disturbing, is the fact that

> Reiki practitioners are taught to submit themselves to the power and influence of other spirits.

By doing so, they become increasingly possessed by them.

By harnessing the energy of 'Rei', and 'channelling' it through their bodies to 'impart' it to others, Reiki practitioners effectively act as mediums. The practice of mediumship is strictly forbidden by scripture (Deut 18:9-14).

Since the spirits Reiki practitioners engage with, divert people's attention away from Jesus, it is clear they are not from God. Consequently it is hardly surprising that many practitioners struggle with physical and mental illness.

Whilst some people claim to have received a measure of healing through Reiki, Jesus tells us that every Kingdom divided against itself will fall (Matt 12:25). So it is unlikely that these people have been truly healed, and much more likely that the nature of their illness changed, e.g. from backache to migraines (or some other condition).

So how can we bring Reiki practitioners into an encounter with the Holy Spirit, and help them back towards God's original plan for their life?

STEP ONE: BUILD A BRIDGE

Most people who pursue Reiki are actually called to a healing ministry. They are misguided, but their heart is simply to help others and see them healed.

When God created them, He put a desire in their hearts for the supernatural, and to see people healed supernaturally. Their desire to heal is a good thing! The problem isn't their desire to heal, but the 'source' they're using, and the method they've chosen.

One way to build a bridge with a Reiki practitioner is to engage in a conversation about healing, or sources. It can also be helpful to let them know that one of the names of our God is Jehovah Rapha – the God who heals us.

Where possible, share some healing experiences that you've witnessed. Being part of a team that God used to release healing, or even witnessing the Holy Spirit bring healing to someone, will add credibility to your story. It's useful to have a list of stories where you can say, "I was there when this happened…"

STEP TWO: LET THEM ENCOUNTER JESUS

If a Reiki practitioner is willing to receive prayer, I would explain that my 'source' is the Spirit of Jesus, obtain their permission to remove the influence of any spirit that's not from a 'true and good' source (i.e. Jesus), and invite the Holy Spirit to bring them into a power encounter with Him.

As a minimum, I would pray for them to be filled with His love and peace, and share any words of knowledge or prophecy the Holy Spirit gave me for them. I would also pray for them to receive physical or emotional healing if required.

Most Reiki practitioners are sensitive to the spiritual realm, and are usually dramatically impacted when they experience the ministry of the Holy Spirit. Often, they'll say:

> *"Wow! I've never felt energy like that before, it feels so pure…"*

> *"That was a really powerful healing. My pain's all gone, I feel so much better…"*

> *"I can just feel so much love…"*

Sometimes these people are so impacted by their encounter, that they want to find out more about the God they've just experienced.

Depending on how the conversation progresses, it may be possible to:

- share the gospel with them,
- explain that when God made them, He put a desire within them to help others and see them healed; and
- let them know there's an opportunity for them to pursue the gift of healing through Christianity, but more importantly for them to start an incredible friendship with an awesome God.

DIALOGUE

The following conversation is typical of some of the conversations I've had with Reiki practitioners in the past.

Sample dialogue: Reiki practitioners	
Me:	*"I understand you have a heart to see people healed?"*
Seeker:	*"Yes, I love helping people and seeing them get better."*
Me:	*"Is that what drew you to Reiki?"*
Seeker:	*"Yes."*
Me:	*"Within Reiki, you invite spiritual guides to help you harness healing energy, don't you?"*
Seeker:	*"Yes, that's right."*
Me:	*"Did you know that when some people*

> *do that, they can have 'bad experiences'*
> *and see spiritual entities they weren't*
> *expecting?*

Seeker: *"Yes, I've heard that can happen", or*
"Yes, that's happened to me before."

Me: *"We've seen lots of people who've had*
those types of experiences.

However, we've been trained to help
people get rid of any negative 'energy',
or 'spirit', and we can introduce you to
the purest and highest Spirit of all – the
Spirit of Jesus. He's the highest spiritual
authority there is."

"We've found that when we partner with
His Spirit to bring healing to people, we
never have a bad encounter."

"Would you like to experience what it
feels like to have the Spirit of Jesus
come and fill you with His love and
peace?"

Seeker: *"Yes, please... I'd love that!"*

Then simply pray for any negative spiritual influence to
be bound in their life, and for the Spirit of Jesus (i.e. the
Holy Spirit) to let them experience something of His love
and power.

If appropriate, you can release words of encouragement
and destiny over their life, for instance:

Me:	*Part of your destiny is to see people healed from all sorts of conditions. That's why you felt such a pull to get involved in spiritual healing. It's part of the call of God on your life.*
	However, there's an invitation today, for you to grow that healing gift through Jesus, the Highest Healing Authority there is. Is that something you'd like to consider?"
Seeker:	*"Who me? But I'm just a first degree Reiki practitioner, I don't think I'm good enough or ready, to ask for His help yet. Would that not be dangerous? Would that not make Him angry or upset? What if He doesn't think I'm good enough, or pure enough?"*
Me:	*"Well I've just been listening to the Spirit of Jesus, and He would love for you to connect directly with Him…"*

Most Reiki Healers are unaware that they can pursue their desire to see others healed through Christianity. Many have a church background, but have become disillusioned (or left) the church because they weren't given any encouragement or opportunity to explore biblical methods of healing.

Over the years, I've seen many of these precious people embrace Jesus and pursue a journey of salvation with Him after having an encounter with His love and power.

STEP 3: NEXT STEPS
Offer suggestions to help them explore Christianity further, or to grow in their friendship with Jesus, e.g. by attending a Christian course on healing.

SPIRITUALISTS AND MEDIUMS

AN OVERVIEW
A spiritualist is one who tries to act as a medium between the living and the dead. This process is sometimes known as 'channelling'. Spiritualists attempt to do this by invoking a spiritual guide to engage with a dead person's spirit, and then sharing any messages they receive back to a person who is still living (often a close friend or relative of the deceased). Spiritualists can often sense, or in some cases 'see' or 'hear' spiritual entities.

CONCERNS
The bible is very clear that we are not to engage in spiritualism (Deut 18:9-14). God does not want us trying to engage with the spirits of dead people, or using any 'spiritual guide', other than the Holy Spirit.

In practice, when spiritualists believe they are engaging with the spirit of a dead person, they are unwittingly communicating with fallen angels (i.e. demons). The 'words' they receive about a dead person's history or background can be accurate, because the spiritual entities they are engaging with may have some awareness of how the deceased person lived their life, and can share that information back to them.

The desire of most spiritualists is to bring comfort and direction to people. Many are unaware that they are engaging with demons.

God's heart is to save these people, bring them into a loving relationship with Jesus Christ, redeem their spiritual sensitivity, and help them find their place within the Body.

However, if you simply tell a spiritualist the things they are doing are wrong, they are likely to react in self-defence, or withdraw. Either way, you will have lost the ability to influence them.

So how can we help people who practice, or engage in, spiritualism encounter Jesus?

STEP ONE: BUILD A BRIDGE

To help a spiritualist encounter Jesus, we can start by looking at the truths they believe, or God-given desires they have, and relate these things back to God's promises, character and power. Then we can encourage them to experience God's goodness, love and power, for themselves.

If I was ministering to a spiritualist, I would let them know that I too believe in the existence of a spiritual realm. I would also affirm their desire to help and comfort people.

During that initial bridge-building conversation, I would agree that God wants us to be spiritually awakened, and highlight the importance of using the right 'source', or 'guide'.

I would also explain that some of the names of God include:

- El Rio, which means the 'God who 'sees'', or the 'God of all revelation' (Gen 16:13);
- The God of all comfort (2 Cor 1:3);
- The God of peace (Judges 6:24); and
- The God who guides us (Is 58:11).

Discussions on sources and guides are likely to gain a spiritualist's attention because most of them, through the process of channelling, will have encountered a 'bad' spiritual experience, which is hardly surprising, given satan's plan to kill, steal and destroy all human life (John 10:10). By opening themselves up to the demonic realm, spiritualists open themselves up to sickness, fear, and other negative manifestations.

DIALOGUE

The following dialogue is typical of the kind of conversations I've had with people from a spiritualist background.

Sample dialogue: spiritualists	
Me:	*"What drew you to spiritualism?"*
Seeker:	*"I've always had an awareness of the spiritual realm, and spiritualism gave me a chance to help me connect with that*

realm."

Me: *"What do you do with that
                   connection?"*

Seeker: *"I get messages for people, so they can
                   feel more at peace, or obtain guidance."*

Me: *"You have a really good heart. It's
                   great that you want to help people."*

                   *"Have you ever had a negative
                   experience whilst channelling, or do you
                   know anyone who has?"*

It would be very surprising for them not to say "yes" to
that question.

Me: *"How did that feel? (or how do you
                   think they must have felt?)"*

Seeker: *"Awful and terrifying."*

Me: *"I've come across lots of people who've
                   had negative experiences. The problem
                   is that when many people access the
                   spirit realm to get messages for people,
                   they've often no idea what kind of spirit-
                   guide they're likely to get, or what
                   impact that spirit will have on their life.*

                   *Did you know that you can ask the Spirit
                   of Jesus to protect you from the
                   influence of negative spirits?"*

Seeker:	*"No... I didn't know that..."*
Me:	*"Yes, one of the names of God is Jehovah-Sabaoth, which means 'The Lord our Protector'. You can also ask Him for comforting words for people and for guidance. Another of His names is Jehovah El-Roi, which means 'the God who sees me, guides me and comforts me."*
	"We've asked the Spirit of Jesus for comforting words, and guidance, for many people. Usually they're overwhelmed (in a good way!) at what He brings. And we know that when we communicate with the Spirit of Jesus, we'll never have a bad experience, because He's altogether good, and completely full of love – both for us and for the people we're looking to help."
Seeker:	*"That's really interesting!"*
Me:	*"Why don't we pray together, and ask the Spirit of Jesus to remove the influence of any negative spirits from your life and let you experience the kind of spiritual revelation He can bring? You've nothing to lose..."*
Seeker:	*"I'd love you to pray for me..."*

Then, with their permission, I would simply invite them to have an encounter with Jesus.

STEP TWO: LET THEM ENCOUNTER JESUS

Over the years, we've seen many spiritualists, and seekers who frequented spiritualists, come to a place of salvation after having had a life-changing encounter with the Holy Spirit.

To bring a spiritualist into an encounter with Jesus, I would re-iterate that our 'source' is the Spirit of Jesus (or the Holy Spirit); forbid the influence of any spirit other than the Holy Spirit from having any influence over them; and invite the Holy Spirit to let them experience something of God's incredible love and peace.

Next, I would ask the Holy Spirit to reveal any words of knowledge, encouragement, wisdom, or prophecy that He wanted to me to share with them.

Because spiritualists are used to communicating with other spiritual beings, when they encounter the purity, love and power of the Holy Spirit (and the messages He brings), they are often overcome. Many of have gone on to receive salvation after such encounters.

> *Note: when sharing the gospel with a spiritualist, it is important to let them know that to pursue friendship with Jesus, they need to let go of all of their other spirit guides. It is important to take time to explain the gospel to them (in simple plain English) and make sure they understand the implications of any decision they might enter into. I've included some guidelines for that in Chapter 7.*

STEP 3: NEXT STEPS

Most spiritualists attend a spiritualist church, or community of people who engage in 'channelling'. If they have chosen to embark on a journey of friendship with Jesus and closed down access to other spirits, they will no longer be able to receive messages for people in the way they used to. They are likely to need a lot of support to help them in their new journey, particularly if they need to leave a community of people they previously felt close to.

It is important to have a regular (welcoming) place of fellowship available, where these new followers of Jesus can grow their faith and feel supported and connected with others.

CAN YOU GET A MESSAGE FROM MY DECEASED LOVED ONE?

Sometimes, people who come for ministry will ask us if we're able to get a message for them from a deceased loved one. Usually these people have had some experience of visiting spiritualists in the past, or know someone who has. Most of the time, they're still grieving for the loss of their loved one, and find it difficult to move on with their life.

In the past, I used to simply shake my head and say *"I'm really sorry, but we don't do that sort of thing here..."* Often they would leave, disappointed, and look for a spiritualist (or medium) who could help them, and thus become more engrained in that form of spirituality.

Now, I take a different approach. I'll start by asking them if they've been to a spiritualist church, or medium, and had a 'reading' done before. Then I'll spend some time listening to their story.

As part of that conversation, I'll explain that people who access the spirit realm, and get messages for people, use 'guides' or 'sources' to help them. I'll also explain that we do things a little differently from the spiritualist church, that our Guide is the Spirit of Jesus (sometimes called the Holy Spirit).

Rather than arguing with them, or telling them spiritualism is wrong (at this point), we start by inviting them to have an encounter with Jesus. Depending on what the Holy Spirit wants to do, or how open they are, we can then build on that encounter, and bring them into a place of love, truth and freedom. As they to start feel loved, accepted and understood, and experience the peace and power of the Holy Spirit, it becomes much easier to share the gospel in a meaningful way with them.

Some of the phrases I might use in a typical dialogue of this kind may include:

> *"Our Guide is the Spirit of Jesus (or the Holy Spirit), and He knows everything about everyone."*

> *"Would it be okay if I asked the Spirit of Jesus if He has a message for you about your mum (or the person they've lost), or the relationship the two of you had? We can also ask if there's any guidance or direction He would like you to have too."*

Then I'd simply invite the Holy Spirit to bring any words of knowledge, encouragement, wisdom, or prophecy that He wanted me to share with the person.

In years of ministering to people in this way, I've rarely encountered anyone who didn't want us to ask Jesus if He had something He wanted to say to them.

Similarly, almost all the people who came expecting a message from a dead relative, and received a word of knowledge or prophecy from the Holy Spirit instead, were impacted in a positive way, and brought closer to Jesus. Many went on to receive salvation and healing.

JENNY'S STORY

We set up some free ministry stalls at a community fair in Ayrshire, and a young married couple came to us. The girl (Jenny) came from a very close family, but had lost her mum a few months before.

Jenny: *"Do you have a message from my mum you could give us?"*

Me: *"Why don't you sit down and we can ask the Spirit of Jesus if there's any message He wants to bring?"*

As I waited on the Holy Spirit, He gave me a really simple, clear message:

> *"Tell Jenny, I saw how well she looked after her mum while she was ill, and tell her that her mum felt*

*incredibly loved and well cared for in the last hours
and minutes of her life."*

As I shared these words with Jenny, she filled up with a
mixture of tears and joy. It transpired that Jenny had taken on
the role of 'main carer' for her mum before she died. Knowing
that her mum felt so loved and well cared for meant so much.

I shared some other words of encouragement and prophecy
with her and towards the end of the session, both Jenny and
Mike (her husband) asked how they too could become
Christians and have a close intimate relationship with Jesus.

You can see from that example, I didn't try to give them a
message from the dead person (!), or argue with them and tell
them it was wrong to ask. I simply invited the Holy Spirit to
reveal whatever message He wanted to share, and as they
encountered Him, they were brought to the place where they
wanted to pursue salvation through Jesus.

CLAIRVOYANTS AND PSYCHICS

AN OVERVIEW

The term clairvoyance is derived from French, with clair
meaning "clear" and voyance meaning "vision". A clairvoyant
is someone who claims to have the ability to perceive things
beyond the natural range of the senses (i.e. extra-sensory
perception). Some also believe they can foretell events through
supernatural intervention (psychic power).

Many clairvoyants discovered their 'gift' after experiencing a traumatic event in their life. Others would say they were born with it. These people usually come from a family line of clairvoyants, where the 'gift' is believed to have been passed down from one generation to another.

Most clairvoyants attempt to use their 'gift' to provide guidance or direction for people. Whilst some practitioners may not recognise that they are interacting with spiritual entities to obtain their 'extra-sensory' information, scripture would suggest they are.

CONCERNS
Clairvoyance is a form of mediumship and is strictly forbidden by scripture (Deut 18:9-14).

So how can we bring a clairvoyant into an encounter with Jesus?

STEP ONE: BUILD A BRIDGE
Because some clairvoyants may refute the fact that they are engaging with spiritual entities to obtain information, it can be difficult to build a bridge they can relate to. Sometimes the best approach is to simply ask them if you can pray for them to encounter Jesus, and trust the Holy Spirit to bring breakthrough.

In some instances though, clairvoyants will have had frightening encounters, and been unable to 'control' the things they saw, or heard, despite their desire to 'turn-off' their 'gift' during the experience. There are countless testimonies where such people have been left feeling tormented or frightened.

If a clairvoyant who'd had a frightening encounter came to me for ministry, I would have a discussion on 'sources', and explain that their experience was most likely caused by liaising (wittingly, or unwittingly) with unclean spirits.

STEP TWO: LET THEM ENCOUNTER JESUS

If they were open to receive ministry, I would ask their permission to remove the influence of any spirit that's not from a 'true and good' source (i.e. Jesus), and explain that our 'source' is the Spirit of Jesus.

I would then ask the Holy Spirit for words of encouragement, prophecy, wisdom or knowledge to share with them, and remain sensitive to His leading.

STEP THREE: NEXT STEPS

It may be appropriate to offer some additional ministry (e.g. SOZO[22], or deliverance) to help them walk into complete freedom especially if they've been practicing as a clairvoyant for a considerable time.

For further information on how to help a clairvoyant have an encounter with Jesus, read the previous section on spiritualists and mediums.

---

[22] SOZO is a Christian ministry that helps people walk into spiritual freedom.

TAROT CARD READERS

OVERVIEW

A tarot card reader is someone who practices divination using tarot cards as a tool to obtain a psychic reading.

When a tarot card reader engages in divination, they partner with demonic spirits (knowingly or unknowingly). They can give very accurate readings about a person's past because they engage with spirits who know things about that person's life. However they have limited access to facts about the future, because God alone knows about things that are still to happen.

If a reader (or someone who's just been to a 'reader') comes for ministry, ask the Holy Spirit to release a combination of words of knowledge and prophetic words about the person's future destiny.

When true prophetic words from God are contrasted with 'readings' given by people engaged in alternative forms of spirituality, the power and purity of God's revelation is far superior to any counterfeits available. And as mentioned previously, when spiritual seekers are brought into an encounter with Jesus, through the Holy Spirit, they usually experience a hunger for more of Him.

ENCOUNTERING JESUS

The process used to bring a tarot card reader into an encounter with Jesus is similar to the approach described for clairvoyants and psychics. It will usually involve a discussion on 'sources', the offer of 'cleansing prayer', and asking the Holy Spirit for words of knowledge (about their past, or current situation) along with words of wisdom or prophecy.

WICCANS

AN OVERVIEW

Wicca is a modern pagan, witchcraft religion. The term Wicca is an 'umbrella' term covering: witchcraft, shamanism and paganism.

Wicca has been cited as one of the fastest growing religions in America[23], and appears to be

> Wicca is one of the fastest growing religions.

particularly attractive to women and teenagers. The take-up of Wicca amongst young people has been so dramatic that some academics are referring to today's youth as the 'Hex Generation'.

Christian writer Marla Alupoaicei[24] interviewed a number of wiccans to find out more about their beliefs. She discovered that prior to becoming wiccans, many of them had a belief in the supernatural and had joined 'The Craft' at a defining moment in time when they were experiencing some sort of emotional crisis. Many became Wiccans because of a sense of pain, fear, or isolation in their life.

By joining The Craft, they hoped they would incur a positive supernatural experience, and be able to harness magical powers

---

[23] American Religious Identification Survey (2003)
[24] Generation Hex: Understanding the Subtle Dangers of Wicca: Dillon Burroughs and Marla Alupoaicei

to help them control the environment around them, thus creating a positive effect in their own life and in the lives of people they care about.

> Many people become Wiccans because they had a traumatic, painful experience

Other reasons people gave for joining Wicca included:

- It's focus on environmentalism (Wiccan is a nature-based religion and many Wiccans feel compassionate about protecting the planet);
- The sense of community offered by people in 'The Craft'; and
- The equal treatment of women and men (in contrast to many religions, which are patriarchal).

Wiccans have no set text like the Christian Bible, but hold to duo-theistic beliefs and worship a moon goddess and horned god.

They believe in the ritual practice of magic and celebrate a number of different festivals throughout the year, including: Halloween, the winter and summer solstice and the autumn and spring solstice. Wiccans claim to practice 'white' magic and would differentiate themselves from 'black' magic, which they associate with evil and satanism.

CONCERNS
The bible is very clear that we should not engage in any sort of sorcery or witchcraft (Deut 18:10-14; 2 Kings 21:6; Rev 22:15).

Scripture also warns against:

- Worshipping nature (Rom 1:25);
- Worshipping other 'gods' (Ex 20:2-3); and
- Communicating with spirits and with the dead, although only some Wiccans engage in this practice (Deut 18:9-12; 2 Chron 33:2-6).

However, as Christians, we need to remember our battle is not against people, but against powers and principalities, and our mission is to reach out to these people with love, and help them come to faith.

So, how can we help someone involved in Wicca to encounter Jesus?

STEP ONE: BUILD A BRIDGE
Over the years, we've prayed and ministered to a number of Wiccans.

The first step in helping them encounter Jesus is to treat them with respect and listen to what they have to say. Most people had no idea what they were getting into when they became wiccans, and are unaware of how harmful it can be.

Few are aware of the incredible Healing Power and Love that can be found through a relationship with Jesus, and many see Christianity as a man-made, powerless, and rule-based, religion.

However there are a few common concepts we can use to try to engage Wiccans in conversation, and encourage them to experience Christian prayer, including:

- We both believe in a spiritual reality;
- We've both experienced the supernatural;
- We both recognise the power of a blood sacrifice (for them that is the highest kind of 'magic' you can invoke, for us the blood of Jesus is also the highest power);
- We both know the supernatural can be harnessed for good or evil; and
- We both believe in healing.

It may also be useful to highlight the great honour and respect Jesus showed women (if speaking to a female Wiccan), and how the bible teaches there is neither male nor female in Christ (Gal 3:28).

It is important to highlight the difference between religion and Christian spirituality and to make them aware of the dynamic spiritual lifestyle that is possible through friendship with Jesus Christ.

As with most other spiritual seekers, there is little point in trying to win Wiccans over through arguments or debate. They need a power encounter with the Holy Spirit.

STEP TWO: LET THEM ENCOUNTER JESUS
Most Wiccans I've encountered have either had a need for healing (physical or emotional), or have a desire to have a dream interpreted.

(a) healing

If a Wiccan asked for healing, I would spend a moment or two explaining that illnesses can have a spiritual root, and ask them if they would be willing to experience some 'cleaning prayer'. If willing, I would bind any negative spiritual influence over their life, pray for God's peace and love to engulf them, and then release healing to them in Jesus' name.

(b) dream interpretation

Two common types of dreams that Wiccans (and other spiritual seekers) often have are:

i.   dreams that terrify them; or
ii. dreams that show them a different path (or spiritual door) they can go through.

Terrifying dreams

If a Wiccan is experiencing terrifying dreams, you can explain that nightmares can come from two main sources: our souls (if we're stressed or frightened about something in the natural realm), or from evil spirits. Either way, leading them through cleansing prayer and inviting the Holy Spirit to let them experience God's love and peace will help create a desire within them to experience more of Jesus and eventually come to a place repentance, deliverance and salvation.

Door dreams

Dreams that show them a different path (or door) are often 'God-dreams', inviting them to receive salvation and pursue their spiritual journey through Jesus.

Note: before attempting to give a biblical interpretation of someone's dream it is important to receive an appropriate level of training[25].

Often after receiving Spirit-led ministry, many Wiccans find themselves hungry to find out more about Jesus and Christian spirituality. If appropriate, explain the gospel to them (in plain English), or engage in an open dialogue about true Christian spirituality and what it means to be follower of Jesus Christ.

Remember it's the Holy Spirit's job to lead someone to salvation. Our job is to partner with Him in that process. People are on a journey, and for some of them the process of coming to the point of salvation can be gradual.

PAGANS AND DRUIDS

Paganism stems from the phrase 'ancient religions' and incorporates many different belief systems, including witchcraft and druid worship. The term 'druid' simply means a Celtic wizard or sorcerer.

You can find out more about building bridges with pagans, and bringing them into an encounter with Jesus by reading the previous section on Wiccans.

---

[25] Recommended courses include (a) Light & Life workshops and training courses on dream interpretation; (b) courses run by 'the Dream House'; and (c) dream training run by North Atlantic Dreams and Streams International.

CONCLUSIONS

Our society is experiencing a spiritual revolution. As people become spiritually awakened, they are experimenting with all sorts of alternatives in an attempt to find a solution to the spiritual hunger they feel. Eight of the most common alternatives seekers have experimented with include:

1. Angel Guides
2. Chi, Chakras, and Aura;
3. Reiki;
4. Spiritualists and Mediums;
5. Clairvoyants and Psychics;
6. Tarot Card Readers;
7. Wiccans; and
8. Pagans

The names of some additional alternative practices are included in Appendix 1, along with an attempt to identify which of the above eight belief systems they most closely align with.

Appendix 2 contains many scriptural names for God. Having an awareness of the different names of God can help you build bridges with seekers and encourage them to have a Holy Spirit encounter.

My prayer is that you will be able to use the principles given in this book, and adapt them for the belief systems held by the people you come into contact with, particularly with those involved in Eastern Mysticism, New Age spirituality, or the occult.

In our experience, when most people are brought into an experiential encounter with Jesus, their preconceptions (and in some instances former dismissal of Christianity) are challenged, and they find themselves drawn to discover what a relationship with Jesus would involve, and what true Christian spirituality has to offer.

For many of these people this will be an on-going process and it is important for them to have a safe environment where they can ask questions, have further encounters with the Holy Spirit, and receive the ministry they need to bring them to a place of healing, freedom and salvation.

The following two Chapters look at how to help seekers start a journey of friendship with Jesus and transition into Kingdom disciples.

REVIEW QUESTIONS AND ACTIVATION EXERCISES

1. What five things will help us build bridges with spiritual seekers?

2. How can we use the names of God to encourage people to have an encounter with Jesus?

3. What 'needs' do the people in your spheres of influence have? Which of these needs link back in with one (or more) of the names of God? Write down your answers.

4. How can offering someone 'cleansing prayer' help them encounter Jesus?

5. How will operating in the spiritual gifts help you bring someone into an encounter with Jesus?

6. Which gifts do you currently operate in, and how confident are you in operating in the spiritual gifts?

7. Put together an action plan to help you become more confident and proficient in these gifts?

8. Ask the Holy Spirit for gifts that you have never walked in. Ask someone who currently operates in those gifts to lay hands on you to receive them. Try practicing them.

9. Embark on some more Holy-Spirit adventures using the bridge-building principles given in this chapter. Record (and share) your experiences.

Chapter seven

FRIENDSHIP WITH JESUS

A s illustrated, it is possible to build bridges with people from alternative spiritual backgrounds and encourage them to have life-changing encounters with Jesus.

Often these people are so impacted they want to find out more about the potential of friendship with Him. Some may still be in an exploratory process, while other may be in a place where they are ready to ask Jesus into their life as Lord and saviour.

STARTING A JOURNEY
If spiritual seeker indicates that they'd like to find out more, you can pray for the Holy Spirit to help them on that journey and direct them to a range of possible options, depending on their preference (see Chapter 8). Often when I've prayed for the Holy Spirit to help people on their journey I've used phrases like:

> *"Let me just pray for the Spirit of wisdom, truth and revelation to guide you, and help you to know which ways are good and which would be unhelpful for you. We can ask Him to give you a sense of peace, when something's okay, and a caution when it's not..."*

If a seeker is open and willing for the Holy Spirit to become their Guide, then often it's only a matter of time before He leads them to a place of salvation.

HELPING A SEEKER RECEIVE SALVATION

Sometimes the person may be in a place where they want to ask Jesus to come into their lives as their Rescuer, Redeemer and Saviour.

If so, spend a few moments explaining the gospel to them in plain English.

Because of the 'synchronistic views' many spiritual seekers hold (i.e. a pick and mix approach with many alternatives), it is important to explain that asking Jesus into their life as Lord, means letting go of all other spirit guides. Jesus needs to be invited into their life as the 'Highest Authority', and as their only God.

It is sometimes useful to use the analogy of marriage when explaining the type of relationship God wants to have with us. On occasions we've given new Christians a little gold ring to keep, as a symbol of the covenant relationship they are entering into.

> *Note: rings are also useful for describing the unfailing love that God offers, i.e. by looking at the unbroken circle, they can be reminded of the fact that God will never stop loving them, even when they make mistakes.*

If a seeker has decided they want to become a follower of Jesus, you can lead them in a short prayer:

- thanking Jesus for making friendship with God possible;
- asking forgiveness for all they things they've done wrong; and
- inviting Jesus into their life as Lord and saviour.

Make sure you also tell any spirit (not from Jesus) to go, pray for them to be filled with the Holy Spirit.

It is also advisable to pray for them to receive the gift of prophecy, so they can grow in their ability to 'hear' God's voice for themself. Often after doing this, I'll ask them to close their eyes, to pray, and to invite the Holy Spirit to reveal a truth from Father God's heart to them. Often they receive an impression or sense of His love, acceptance, affirmation or other revelation, which can be confirmed through scripture.

When this happens, I'll take a few moments to show them where the revelation they've just shared can be found in the Bible.

As you draw your ministry session to a close, make sure you exchange contact information with them, and provide them with opportunities for growing in their new-found faith.

BUT I DON'T WANT TO GIVE UP MY SPIRIT GUIDE!
What if someone wants to embark on friendship with Jesus, but doesn't want to give up their spirit guide, or angel?

Explain that Jesus won't ask them to give up anything that's good for them. Encourage them to pray and to ask the Holy Spirit to show them what He wants them to do.

Often when people do this, they receive reassurance that the 'new path' they're embarking on is far superior to the one they've been on, and become willing to let go of any previous guides.

If they are still not keen to give up their spirit guide, explain that God has given us the scriptures to help us develop our relationship with Him. Explain that they state it's the Holy Spirit's role, to guide us (John 16:13), and that other guides can be deceiving and dangerous.

REVIEW QUESTIONS AND ACTIVATION EXERCISES

1. If a spiritual seeker indicates that they'd like to explore Christianity further, how might you pray for them?

2. Many seekers have a synchronistic approach to their spirituality. What sort of discussion should you have with them if they express a desire to become a follower of Jesus?

3. How can the analogy of marriage, and the symbolic use of a ring, help you share the Gospel with a seeker?

4. The key to sharing God's love effectively with spiritual seekers, is to remain sensitive to the Holy Spirit's leading. Having a pure heart will increase your ability to communicate with God.

   Spend some time in worship and ask God to search your heart to see if there is anything in your life that could get in the way of being led by Holy Spirit. Repent from any wrong actions or behaviours He highlights to you.

5. Ask the Holy Spirit to fill you and help you see your circumstances from Heaven's perspective.

6. Look for more opportunities to have Holy Spirit adventures. Record your experiences.

7. Ask the Holy Spirit to bring you alongside someone who is ready to start a relationship with Jesus and use the principles outlined in this chapter to help them do that.

Chapter eight

WHAT NEXT?

The previous chapters show how it is possible to build bridges with spiritual seekers and encourage them to have their own face-to-face encounter with Jesus. Once they do this, many of them are so impacted by God's love, power and grace, that they are keen to start a journey of friendship with Him, or explore more about what it means to be a follower of Jesus.

So how do we help spiritual seekers, who've had life-changing encounters with Jesus, grow in their new-found faith and transition into Kingdom disciples? Especially, when most of these new Christians are more spiritually aware of the supernatural realm around them, than many Christians, who have been attending churches for decades!

To answer that question, we need to remind ourselves of what these seekers are looking for, and of what it was that drew them into an encounter with Jesus in the first place.

A REMINDER... WHAT ARE SEEKERS LOOKING FOR?
Spiritual seekers are looking for different things including:

1. Healing;
2. Guidance;
3. Comfort;
4. Peace;
5. Love; and
6. Acceptance.

In addition, most (although not all) are looking for a community of people they can feel part of, and explore their spirituality in a safe environment. A place where they feel loved and accepted, without fear of condemnation or criticism.

Most are looking for emotional, experiential, connections, rather than intellectual ones, and will prefer an environment where they can play an active part in their spiritual development and growth.

SALLY'S STORY
'Sally' was a practitioner of 'psychic spiritual healing'. However she had an injury in her ankle that caused her considerable pain. Despite trying different treatments (including psychic healing), nothing had worked and she was left in agony.

She came along to one of our events to try some of our 'free healing prayer'. As the team started to pray for her, the Holy Spirit filled her with a tangible sense of His love and warmth, and she was instantly healed. Visibly shocked, she stood to her feet and started testing her ankle...

"I can't believe this, it's healed! How did you do that?"

Our team explained that Jesus had healed her, and the power she felt flowing through her was His Spirit. Within minutes, she was 'grilling them' about this 'God', and before long asked to start a journey of friendship with Him too. She was so impacted, that she spent the rest of the day as an 'on-site' missionary, directing people to our stall because:

"They're operating with a power much greater than anything I've ever seen!"

Sally was keen to grow in her new-found faith, and learn all she could about following Jesus, so we arranged to meet with her the following week.

However, we had no experience, and little idea, about how to disciple someone like Sally. Most of us were 'good, evangelical Christians', and so it seemed the obvious choice to introduce Sally to the scriptures and do an introductory bible study on 'What it meant to be a Christian' with her. In our ignorance, we also produced a long list of 'do's and 'don'ts', and detailed explanations on why alternative forms of spirituality were wrong.

As we sat round the table and began our 'preach', Sally looked puzzled, then as her disappointment and frustration grew, she exclaimed…

"I think I've heard enough! This isn't what I expected at all... This is 'religious', not 'spiritual', and 'intellectual', not 'emotional'!

A few moments later she got up to leave. We were taken aback, and I doubt that any of us present will ever forget the experience (or embarrassment we felt).

So where did we go wrong?

Thankfully, Sally was gracious enough to give us some further feedback.

Sally had come to faith in Jesus just the week before, through an authentic, experiential encounter. As she experienced the reality of His love and His healing, she knew, beyond doubt that Jesus Christ was real. She was desperate to grow the relationship with Him, to get to know Him, and she wanted to be part of a community that would help her do that.

But she was looking to grow a friendship with the Person of Jesus, not join a religion. The community she longed for was one that was non-judgemental, open, trustworthy and allowed her to participate by asking questions (without fear of reprimand), and to engage in experiential encounters.

In contrast she found our approach of asking her to sit and listen, whilst we preached and turned pages of the bible to 'prove' points, unhelpful. Instead of just 'sitting and listening', she wanted to contribute, to feel like a valued part of a family, rather than a 'wayward school girl'.

Having brought Sally into a spiritual encounter with Jesus, we were attempting to disciple her in a way that she perceived was: arrogant, rigid, prescriptive, judgemental, intellectual and boring! It was a humbling encounter! I was reminded of the Apostle Paul's letter to the church at Galatia:

> *'Having started in the Spirit, are you now ending up with the flesh?' (Gal 3:3)*

In reflection, we should have taken some time to get to know Sally as a person, looked to see what God was already doing in her life, and started there, rather than simply trying to impose our ideas on her.

WILMA'S STORY

In contrast, Wilma had a background in spiritualism and had flirted with some aspects of Wicca. She came to one of our events in search of physical healing.

Like Sally, she experienced God's healing power when the team prayed for her. Her symptoms completely disappeared and she was completely engulfed in the Father's love. Tearfully, she sat in God's Presence, asking forgiveness for the things she had done wrong in her life and invited Jesus to become her Lord and Saviour.

Wilma was invited to join a local study group (which she loved), and a few months later, was publically baptised in front of her family and friends. She is still growing steadily in her faith.

So why did the approach taken with Wilma work, whilst our efforts to disciple Sally met with failure - despite the fact that both used a similar method?

It is because people are individuals, with different preferences and learning styles, and 'one-size' doesn't fit all.

> People are individuals, 'one-size doesn't fit all'.

For some people (particularly those with some previous church background or affiliation), participating in bible studies, or courses like Alpha, are ideal.

But, most spiritual seekers are not looking for an 'intellectual' way of developing their new-found faith. They are looking for a participative, experientially-based approach, where they are brought into encounters with the Person of Jesus, through the Holy Spirit, and then taught how those encounters relate to God's character, and to scripture. They are also looking to be part of a larger family, where they can pursue an authentic, spiritual and supernatural lifestyle.

Today, I purposely take time to find out what kind of 'follow-up' will work for different people, and then attempt to direct them to a discipleship environment that will 'fit' their needs.

For most, this will include 'encounter services' (or classes), where they experience the Presence of God, are taught through participative discussions, or attend workshops on topics like:

- Christian meditation;
- The God who loves;
- The God who speaks;
- The God who speaks through dreams and visions;
- The God who heals;
- The God who sets us free;
- The God who forgives;
- Our supernatural calling and destiny;
- Our spiritual DNA;
- Partnering with the Spirit of Jesus;
- Heaven's idea of community;
- Why we worship; and
- Why we pray.

The key is to:

> Find ways of communicating the Christian message to people, in authentic, powerful, ways that they can connect with, and relate to.

Then we can look for ways to teach the truths of scripture using their God-given hunger as a platform to build on. I've included some useful resources that can assist with this in Appendix Three.

As we implement an 'experience-led' approach to discipleship, we need to be careful not to present a diluted message of the gospel, by omitting key topics (such as holiness, or sin). However, should try to communicate them in a sensitive, Spirit-led, way that doesn't deliberately alienate people.

> *Note: On some occasions people will be offended at the message of the Gospel. This is unavoidable. However we can avoid presenting it to them in a judgemental, Pharisaic, way which causes unnecessary offence.*

If we alienate people, we lose the ability to influence them, and if we do that, we won't be able to disciple them.

LIFE FORCE

My friends, Becky and Daniel Frank are church planters in the East-End of Glasgow. They are also leaders of our local Light and Life outreach team for that area.

The way they've set about planting their church, and discipling new believers, exemplifies an approach I believe we all need to consider. They host several outreach events per year in their local area, where members of the community are invited to sample different aspects of Christian spirituality (i.e. prophecy, healing, dream interpretation etc.).

Then they follow-up those who want to explore Christian spirituality further (including new believers), by holding 'encounter meetings' (called Life Force) over several weeks. These 'encounter meetings' are used to bring people into repeated encounters with the Holy Spirit, whilst at the same time teaching them biblical principles for developing their relationship with Jesus.

In addition to holding meetings, Becky and Daniel have also taken time to 'do life' with the community of people who have gathered around them – thus creating an authentic sense of family.

Their approach has been so successful that many people, who have come to faith through the outreach events and discipleship process, are now active members of their outreach and discipleship teams.

Because of the success they've experienced, people have asked them for the 'secret recipe' behind 'Life Force', so they can apply it to their own community. Do you want to know what that secret recipe is?

I asked Becky and she responded:

> *"Spend time praying about the unmet needs of your community, and then ask the Holy Spirit for a strategy to meet those needs."*
>
> *"There's no 'one-size' fit's all, and no 'cookie cutters' in the Kingdom."*

THE GATHERING

Rex Allchurch is a young man who is also in the process of planting a church called 'The Gathering', in Cowplain, near Portsmouth. Aimed predominately at young people between 15 and 30 years old, Rex has seen his group grow and forge into an authentic community of people, who are at different stages in their walk with God.

Some of these people come from broken, impoverished, homes, whilst others are from secure church-going families.

Rex's vision is to create a safe environment where people can encounter the God of the Bible through genuine, powerful, Holy Spirit encounters. And as they've met together in an atmosphere of worship, our God has not disappointed!

Prophetic words, healings and miracles have become common place and over a period of five months, the group has expanded from a handful of people, into a community of between 50 and 70 folk.

I asked Rex for some pointers on 'how he did church', and he responded:

> *"Don't hold back. Go after the full, manifest Presence of God. Some people try to attract young people by putting on professional stage performances with 'cool' music and other attractions, and whilst these things may bring young people in, it won't keep them. They need to encounter the manifest Presence of God – that's what they're hungry for (even if they don't realise it)."*

'Services' at The Gathering are stripped back and simple. They worship, give a short message, and allow the Holy Spirit to move. The results are changed lives, and an impassioned group of people. Everyone has an opportunity to participate, and the 'teaching programme' is put together to address questions people in the group have raised, including:

"What (or who) is the Holy Spirit?"
"What is prayer, and how do we do it?"

In addition, they cover controversial and topical headlines on subjects such as homosexuality, the recession, and other issues.

Like Becky and Daniel, Rex's approach to discipling new believers is to 'do life' with them and take them on adventures. These adventures include outreach visits to the local prison, where they share up-to-date testimonies and see many inmates brought to faith. They also include learning to partner with the Holy Spirit and see the Kingdom of God released through prophecy, healing and miracles.

SOME THOUGHTS

The approach Becky, Daniel and Rex have taken to 'doing church' sounds a lot like the way Jesus discipled His followers. He 'shared life' with them, took them on adventures, created space for them to ask questions, taught them the scriptures, and showed them how to partner with the Holy Spirit and see the Kingdom of God released - with breath-taking effect.

This 'Jesus-pattern' was replicated in the early church, and the Book of Acts informs us that the first Christians shared life together, went on adventures, and operated in signs, wonders and miracles. They also embraced an authentic lifestyle by challenging traditions and outward signs of religion (for

instance, the teaching that gentiles should be circumcised).
Instead they brought the Spirit and the Word together, and
pursued relationships with the Living God and with each other.

The first Chapter of this book is entitled '*Get Ready for a
Revolution*'. Throughout history, revolutions have re-shaped
the way communities and societies have functioned. For
instance, the Agricultural and Industrial Revolutions reshaped
the way society lived and worked. Similarly the French
revolution re-shaped the structure of society within France

The heart-felt desire of many spiritual seekers to have
'authentic spiritual encounters' in communities where they feel
loved and accepted (as opposed to simply engaging in religious
rituals), aligns closely with God's heart for a vibrant, dynamic,
grace-based, power-filled, Church.

Could it be that this spiritual revolution will re-shape the future
outlook of much of the Church, and herald a return to the blueprint given in the Book of Acts?

I hope it does!

REVIEW QUESTIONS AND ACTIVATION EXERCISES

1. What are some of the things that spiritual seekers are looking for?

2. How does your group, church or organisation, currently tailor discipleship activities to meet their needs?

3. What changes can you make in your discipleship approach to help new Christians (with an alternative spiritual background) transition into Kingdom disciples?

4. What is your greatest fear in stepping out and bringing people into encounters with Jesus?

5. What steps can you take to overcome that fear?

6. Spend some time in worship and ask the Holy Spirit to give you a glimpse of what your community would look like if it was saturated with God's Presence. Pray for His incredible Presence to intensify wherever He leads you.

7. Speak the following declarations over your life:

   a) I am God's friend, and His ambassador.
   b) My life is a powerful instrument for God's Kingdom.
   c) My prayers are powerful and effective.
   d) I expect to have powerful, God-encounters, with people today.
   e) Multitudes will be in heaven because of my life.

8. Read through the Book of Acts and write down everything the Holy Spirit shows you about God's heart for His Church, and for an authentic community of believers. If you are part of a study group, discuss your answers with each other.

9. What can you do, to help make that vision a reality in your own life, and in the lives of the people you lead, or have influence over? Write down your answer.

10. Put together an action plan, based on your answer to question 9.

11. Say 'yes' to Jesus! Pray and take practical steps to make that vision a reality.

CONCLUSIONS

We live in some of the most exciting days since the very beginning of time. God has created a spiritual hunger in the hearts of ordinary people, and in parallel, has orchestrated a climate where it is easier than it has ever been before to step out and share His love with a lost and dying world, through: love, prophecy, healing, signs, wonders and miracles.

This book provides keys to help you engage with a spiritually awakened society, bring them into encounters with Jesus, and help usher in the largest revival the world has ever seen. It also provides some cultural considerations we need to think about, if we want to see these newly awakened seekers brought to a place of salvation, and transition into Kingdom disciples.

All creation is waiting for our response. Seize the moment! Say '*yes*' and allow Jesus to take you on the most amazing adventures. As you engage with a spiritually awakened society, partner with the Holy Spirit, and see His lost kids brought into face-to-face encounters with Him, you will become part of a growing throng of people who are seeing our nation(s) changed – one person, and one family, at a time.

Go for it! And feel free to send me your stories! I'd love to hear how you get on.

Happy adventuring!

Barbara

BIBLIOGRAPHY

A practical guide to supernatural evangelism; Chris Overstreet.

Basic Training for the Prophetic Ministry: Kris Vallotton.

Christianity after religion; Dianna Butler Bass

Comparison of church attendance trends in the UK and Australia, Christian Research Association (2000).

Dreams, a biblical model of interpretation by Jim Driscoll and Zach Mapes.

Equipping your church in a spiritual age; Steve Hollinghurst, Yvonne Richmond and Roger Whitehead.

Evangelism in a Spiritual Age; Steven Croft, Anne Richmond, Rob Frost, Yvonne Richmond, Mark Ireland and Nick Spencer.

Generation Hex; Dillon Burroughs, Marla Alupoaicei

GPs using complementary and alternative therapies; Rebecca Wallersteiner.

God talks to me in my dreams: the occurrence and significance of children's dreams about God, International Journal of Children's spirituality (2001) by Kate Adams.

Life to the Full by Steven Anderson and James Renwick

Light and Life training and resources: www.lightlife.org.uk

Mintel report on complementary medicines in the UK: Dec 2009.

New Research Explores Teenage Views and Behaviour Regarding the Supernatural, Barna Update, January 23, 2006.

North Atlantic Dreams courses on prophecy and dream interpretation: www.northatlanticdreams.net

Practical application of spiritual intelligence in the workplace, Human Resource Management International Digest (2006).

Releasing Healing, by Steven Anderson

Sharing God's Love through Prophecy and the Revelatory Gifts, by Barbara Jenkinson available from www.lightlife.org.uk

Survey Amongst Teenage Girls (1997), Social Issues Research Centre, Kate Fox

The Dream House: www.thedreamhouse.co

The Limit Experience of Senior High School Pupils: a study across four Catholic Schools. PHD Thesis, Fitzroy Vic, Australian Catholic University (2001) by Paul McQuillan.

The rise of mind-body-soul publishing, Journal of Alternative Spiritualties and New Age Studies; Elizabeth Puttick.

The Perfect Storm, by Sebastian Junger.

The Source: www.sourcelife.net

The Spiritual Revolution, Paul Heelas and Linda Woodhead.

The Spirituality of adults in Britain, Scottish Journal of Healthcare Chaplaincy (2002) by David Hay.

When Heaven Invades Earth, by Bill Johnson

Appendix One

GLOSSARY OF TERMS

Term	Definition
Acupuncture	A form of treatment used in traditional Chinese medicine. It is based on the belief that there are energetic pathways (Rei), or channels, throughout the body associated with internal organs and structures. More information on Rei can be found in the section on Rei, Chakras &Auras on Pg 79.
Angel Guides	Guides used by New Age practitioners and Eastern Mystics. More information on Angel guides can be found on Pg 71.
Astrology	The study of celestial bodies in an attempt to foretell future events. Read the Section on clairvoyants and psychics on Pg 100 for further information.
Aura	New Age practitioners define 'Aura' as the 'energy life force' that surrounds objects and life forms. More information on Aura can be found in the section on Rei, Chakras &Auras on Pg 79

Chakras	New Age practitioners believe there are seven points in the human body (called Chakras) through which 'Chi' can be received. More information on Chakras can be found in the section on Rei, Chakras &Auras on Pg 79
Channelling	Channelling is a term used for accessing energy or information from the spiritual realm through spirit guides and passing that energy or information onto others. See section on Spiritualists and Mediums on Pg 91.
Chi	New Age practitioners believe Chi to be the 'energy life flow' that flows through all creation. More information on Chi can be found in the section on Rei, Chakras & Auras on Pg 79.
Clairvoyant	The term clairvoyant is derived from French, with clair meaning 'clear' and voyance meaning 'vision'. A clairvoyant is someone who claims to have the ability to perceive things beyond the natural range of the senses. Some also believe they can foretell events using psychic power. See section on Pg 100 for further information.
Complementary and alternative health	Alternative health definition: a variety of therapeutic or preventative health care practices, such as homeopathy, naturopathy and herbal medicine, that do not follow generally accepted medical methods.

Destiny Word	An alternative phrase sometimes used by our teams for 'prophecy'.
Druid	The term 'druid' means Celtic wizard or sorcerer. See section on Pg 109 for further information.
Medium	A medium is someone who attempts to obtain messages from the spirits of dead people. See section on mediums on Pg 91 for further information.
National Federation of Spiritual Healers	An organisation of psychic healers. See section on Pg 100 for further information.
Pagan	The term 'pagan' stems from the phrase 'ancient religions' and it incorporates many different belief systems including witchcraft and druid worship. See section on Pg109 for further information.
Psychics	Psychics believe people have a 'sixth' sense that they can use to communicate telepathically with objects or people. See section on Pg 100 for further information.
Rei	Rei is another name given to 'Chi'. More information on Rei can be found in the section on Rei, Chakras &Auras on Pg 79
Reiki	A Reiki practitioner is someone who tries to harness healing energy from 'Rei' and impart it to others. See Section on Pg 83 for further information.

Spiritual reading	An alternative phrase sometimes used by our teams for prophecy.
SOZO	A Christian healing practice. The name SOZO means 'saved, healed and delivered'.
Spiritualist	A spiritualist is someone who tries to act as a medium between the living and the dead. See section on Pg 91 for further information.
Tarot card reader	A tarot card reader is someone who engages in divination using tarot cards as a tool to obtain psychic readings. See section on Pg 103 for further information.
The Craft	A term synonymous with Wicca. See Pg 104
Wicca	Wicca is a modern pagan, witchcraft religion. The term 'Wicca' is an umbrella term covering: witchcraft, shamanism and paganism. See Pg 104 for further information.
Yoga	A Hindu discipline aimed at training the consciousness for a state of perfect spiritual insight and tranquillity. Read the section on Reiki for further insight on Pg 83.

Appendix Two

Names of God

Old Testament Name	Definition
Adonai	A reference to the Lordship of God (Mal 1:6)
El-Elyon	The most high God (Gen 14:17-20, Is 14:13-14)
El-Olam	Meaning "The everlasting God" (Is 40:28-31)
El-Roi	The strong one who sees (Gen 16:13)
El-Shaddai	The God of the mountains or God Almighty (Gen 17:1, Ps 91:1)
Elohim	God of power and might. (Gen 1:1; Ps 19:1)
Jehovah Gmolah	The God of Recompense (Jer 51:6)
Jehovah Jireh	The Lord will provide (Gen 22:13-14)
Jehovah Maccaddeshem	The Lord your sanctifier (Ex 31:13)

Jehovah Nissi	The Lord our banner (Ex 17:15)
Jehovah Rapha	The Lord our healer (Ex 15:26)
Jehovah Rohi	The Lord my shepherd (Ps 23:1)
Jehovah Sabbaoth	The Lord of Hosts and our Protector (Is 6:1-3)
Jehovah Shalom	The Lord is peace (Jud 6:24)
Jehovah Shammah	The Lord who is present (Ez 48:35)
Jehovah Tsidkenu	The Lord our righteousness (Jer 23:6)
Jehovah Yahweh	The Lord who saves us (Gen 2:4)

More names of God: Father, Son, Holy Spirit

Avenger	1Thess 4:6
Almighty	Genesis 17:1
All in all	Colossians 3:11
Alpha	Revelation 22:13
Amen	Revelation 3:14
Ancient of days	Daniel 7:9
Anointed One	Psalm 2:2
Apostle	Hebrews 3:1
Arm of the Lord	Isaiah 53:1
Author of eternal salvation	Hebrews 5:9
Author of our faith	Hebrews 12:2
Author of peace	1 Cor. 14:33
Beginning	Revelation 21:6

Branch	Jeremiah 33:15
Bread of God	John 6:33
Bread of life	John 6:35
Breath of life	Genesis 2:7, Revelation 11:11
Bridegroom	Isaiah 62:5
Bright morning star	Revelation 22:16
Captain of salvation	Hebrews 2:10
Carpenter	Mark 6:3
Chief shepherd	1 Peter 5:4
Chosen One	Isaiah 42:1
Christ	Matthew 22:42
Christ of God	Luke 9:20
Christ the Lord	Luke 2:11
Christ, son of the Living God	Matthew 16:16
Comforter	John 14:26(kjv)
Commander	Isaiah 55:4
Consuming fire	Deut. 4:24, Heb. 12:29
Cornerstone	Isaiah 28:16
Counsellor	Isaiah 9:6
Creator	1 Peter 4:19
Crown of beauty	Isaiah 28:5
Dayspring	Luke 1:78
Deliverer	Romans 11:26
Desired of all nation	Haggai 2:7
Diadem of beauty	Isaiah 28:5
Door	John 10:7(kjv)
Dwelling place	Psalm 90:1
Elect one	Isaiah 42:1
Emmanuel	Matthew 1:23(kjv)
End	Revelation 21:6
Eternal God	Deut. 33:27

Eternal life	1 John 5:20
Eternal Spirit	Hebrews 9:14
Everlasting Father	Isaiah 9:6
Everlasting God	Genesis 21:33
Excellent	Psalm 148:13(kjv)
Faithful and true	Revelation 19:11
Faithful witness	Revelation 1:5
Father	Matthew 6:9
Fortress	Jeremiah 16:19
Foundation	1 Cor. 3:11
Fountain of living waters	Jeremiah 2:13
Friend	Matthew 11:19
Gentle whisper	1 Kings 19:12
Gift of God	John 4:10
Glory of the Lord	Isaiah 40:5
God Almighty	Genesis 17:1
God of the whole earth	Isaiah 54:5
God over all	Romans 9:5
God who sees me	Genesis 16:13
Goodness	Psalm 144:2(kjv)
Good Shepherd	John 10:11
Governor	Psalm 22:28(kjv)
Great High Priest	Hebrews 4:14
Great Shepherd	Hebrews 13:20
Guide	Psalm 48:14
Head of the Body	Colossians 1:18
Head of the Church	Ephesians 5:23
Hiding place	Psalm 32:7
Highest	Luke 1:76
High Priest forever	Hebrews 6:20
Holy Ghost	John 14:26
Holy One	Acts 2:27

Holy One of Israel	Isaiah 49:7
Holy Spirit	John 15:26
Hope	Titus 2:13
Horn of salvation	Luke 1:69
Husband	Isaiah 54:5, Hosea 2:16
I AM	Exodus 3:14, John 8:58
Immanuel	Isaiah 7:14
Intercessor	Rom 8:26,27,34 Heb 7:25
Jealous	Exodus 34:14(kjv)
Jehovah	Psalm 83:18(kjv)
Jesus	Matthew 1:21
Judge	Isaiah 33:22, Acts 10:42
Just One	Acts 22:14
Keeper	Psalm 121:5
King	Zechariah 9:9
King Eternal	1 Timothy 1:17
King Of Glory	Psalm 24:10
King of Jews	Matthew 27:11
King of Kings	1 Timothy 6:15
King of Saints	Revelation 15:3
Lamb of God	John 1:29
Last Adam	1 Cor. 15:45
Lawgiver	Isaiah 33:22
Leader	Isaiah 55:4
Life	John 14:6
Light of the World	John 8:12
Like an Eagle	Deut. 32:11
Lily of the Valleys	Song 2:1
Lion of the tribe of Judah	Revelation 5:5
Living God	Daniel 6:20
Living Stone	1 Peter 2:4

Living Water	John 4:10
Lord of all	Acts 10:36
Lord of Glory	1 Cor. 2:8
Lord of Harvest	Matthew 9:38
Lord of Hosts	Haggai 1:5
Lord of Lords	1 Tim. 6:15
Lord our Righteousness	Jeremiah 23:6
Love	1 John 4:8
Maker	Job 35:10, Psalm 95:6
Majesty on high	Hebrews 1:3
Man of sorrows	Isaiah 53:3
Master	Luke 5:5
Mediator	1 Timothy 2:5
Merciful God	Jeremiah 3:12
Messenger of the Covenant	Malachi 3:1
Messiah	John 4:25
Mighty God	Isaiah 9:6
Mighty One	Isaiah 60:16
Nazarene	Matthew 2:23
Offspring of David	Revelation 22:16
Omega	Revelation 22:13
Only begotten Son	John 1:18(kjv)
Our Passover lamb	1 Cor. 5:7
Our peace	Ephesians 2:14
Physician	Luke 4:23
Portion	Psalm 73:26,Psalm 119:57
Potter	Isaiah 64:8
Power of God	1 Cor. 1:24
Prince of Peace	Acts 3:15
Prophet	Acts 3:22
Purifier	Malachi 3:3

Quickening Spirit	1 Corinthians 15:45(kjv)
Rabboni (teacher)	John 20:16
Radiance of God's Glory	Heb.1:3
Redeemer	Job 19:25
Refiner's Fire	Malachi 3:2
Refuge	Jeremiah 16:19
Resurrection	John 11:25
Rewarder	Hebrews 11:6
Righteous One	1 John 2:1
Rock	1 Cor.10:4
Root of David	Rev. 22:16
Rose of Sharon	Song 2:1
Ruler of God's Creation	Rev. 3:14
Ruler over Kings of the earth	Rev 1:5
Ruler over Israel	Micah 5:2
Saviour	Luke 2:11
Sceptre	Numbers 24:17
Seed	Genesis 3:15
Servant	Isaiah 42:1
Shade	Psalm 121:5
Shepherd of our Souls	1Peter 2:25
Shield	Genesis 15:1
Son of David	Matthew 1:1
Song	Exodus 15:2, Isaiah 12:2
Son of God	Matthew 27:54
Son of Man	Matthew 8:20
Son of the Most High	Luke 1:32
Spirit of Adoption	Romans 8:15
Spirit	John 4:24
Spirit of God	Genesis 1:2
Spirit of truth	John 14:17,15:26,16:13

Strength	Jeremiah 16:19
Stronghold	Nahum 1:7
Strong Tower	Proverbs 18:10
Sun of Righteousness	Malachi 4:2
Teacher	John 13:13
True Light	John 1:9
True Witness	Revelation 3:14
Truth	John 14:6
Vine	John 15:5
Wall of fire	Zechariah 2:5
Way	John 14:6
Wisdom of God	1 Cor. 1:24
Witness	Isaiah 55:4
Wonderful	Isaiah 9:6
Word	John 1:1
Word of God	Revelation 19:13
Yah	Isaiah 12:2(kjv),Psalm 68:4(nkjv)

Appendix Three

Useful Resources

Dreams, a biblical model of interpretation by Jim Driscoll and Zach Mapes.

Equipping your church in a spiritual age; Steve Hollinghurst, Yvonne Richmond and Roger Whitehead.

Healing Rooms Training: www.healingrooms-scotland.com

Life to the Full by Steven Anderson and James Renwick

Light and Life training and resources: www.lightlife.org.uk

North Atlantic Dreams courses on prophecy and dream interpretation: www.northatlanticdreams.net

Speaking their language (available on Amazon) by Heather Sutherland

The Dream House: www.thedreamhouse.co

The Source: www.sourcelife.net

The Total Wellbeing Network: www.navatherapy.org.uk

OTHER PUBLICATIONS BY THE AUTHOR

CONTACT INFORMATION

Barbara Jenkinson
Light and Life

Web address: www.lightlife.org.uk
Email: info@lightlife.org.uk

SHARING GOD'S LOVE
Through Prophecy and the Revelatory Gifts

By Barbara Jenkinson

This book will take you on an incredible journey with the Holy Spirit as you develop your prophetic gifting.

Learn:
- About God's heart for His lost children;
- How to use prophecy and the revelatory gifts to share God's love;
- How to activate and grow:
  o In your gift of prophecy;
  o In the word of knowledge;
  o In the word of wisdom;
  o In the gift of discerning of spirits;
- How to overcome obstacles and doubt.

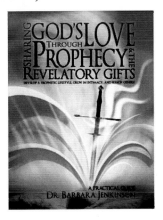

Complete with true and inspiring stories, each chapter contains review questions, activation exercises and a personal journal to record your progress and experiences.

Expect: your relationship with the Holy Spirit to rise to a new level; to grow in confidence; and ability to share the Father's heart with others through prophecy and the revelatory gifts.

Suitable for: personal study, and as a resource for churches, organisations and small groups.

INTERMEDIATE MENTORING SCHOOL

By Barbara Jenkinson and Anne Watkins

Grow in confidence and gifting, and fully possess all God has for your life!

This school will help you:

1. **Embrace the Anointing**, and release the Kingdom of Heaven through signs, wonders and miracles.
2. **Communicate with God**, and sharpen your ability to partner with His Holy Spirit.
3. **Overcome Spiritual Plateaus**, and fully possess your spiritual inheritance.
4. **Look and Look Again**, and discover biblical secrets for unpacking prophecy and releasing words of knowledge.
5. **Release Healing**, using proven biblical principles.
6. **Stand on the Shoulders of Giants**, obtain a biblical understanding of mantles and impartations. Identify areas in your life where God wants to release a fresh anointing, and accelerate your gifting.

Includes links to audio teaching for each topic.

Suitable for: personal study, and as a resource for churches, organisations and small groups.

A BOOK OF MIRACLES

*Some Adventures of God and His Kids
in Scotland (& beyond)*

By Barbara Jenkinson

It's been utterly mind blowing to see our amazing God at work in Scotland (and beyond), these last months and years.

I've put this manuscript together as a reminder of the miracles we've seen Him do – both through Light & Life and in our personal lives.

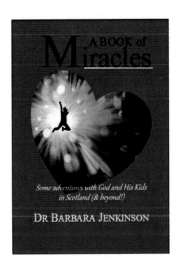

Sometimes it's all too easy to lose sight of how awesome, faithful and loving He is.

It's my prayer that whoever reads these pages will be encouraged, have their faith strengthened, and fall more in love with our incredible Jesus.

Due to be published soon.

LIGHT AND LIFE TRAINING

We run training courses to activate, release and equip people in prophetic evangelism on a regular basis. On our courses you can learn how to develop a lifestyle of intimacy with the Holy Spirit, and share God's love with others through:

- o The Jesus model of healing;
- o Prophecy;
- o Biblical methods of dream interpretation;
- o Touch (simple head, shoulder and hand massage, combined with prayer and prophecy);
- o Prophetic art;
- o Creative evangelism (balloon sculpting, face-painting etc.)

For further information visit our website: www.lightlife.org.uk, or contact us by:

Email: info@lightlife.org.uk
Phone: 07792 102 469